P9-DJK-772

REJOICE WITH US

MEMBERSHIP RESOURCE BOOK

Written and compiled by

NORMAN WEGMEYER AND GLENN WEGMEYER

Edited by ROBERT HOYER

Copyright © 1972

AUGSBURG PUBLISHING HOUSE

BOARD OF PUBLICATION OF THE
LUTHERAN CHURCH IN AMERICA

CONCORDIA PUBLISHING HOUSE

Prepared for the Boards of Parish Education of the
Lutheran Church in America, The Lutheran Church—
Missouri Synod, and The American Lutheran Church.

ISBN 0-570-03508-2

PHOTO CREDITS:

Page 12—DeWys, Inc.; Pages 16, 22, 24, 26, 55,
67, 123, 128, 129, 139—Bob Combs; Page 18—
Blair Seitz; Pages 21, 30, 34, 52, 74, 87, 103, 104,
107, 127, 130—Wallowitch; Page 37—Concordia;
Page 42—K. Webster; Pages 45, 64, 85—Paul
Ockrassa; Pages 59, 68—Greer Cavagnaro; Page
77—DeWys, Inc.; Pages 90, 100, 119, 145, 147—
Joseph Zimbrolt; Page 97—Mark Brokering; Page
112—Rohn Engh; Page 115—Tri City Photo, Inc.;
Page 120—Sister Noemi Weygant; Page 125—Don
Knight; Page 136—Mrs. Lila G. Scrimsher; Page
141—State Health Dept.

Cover Design—Betty Wind

Contents

Foreword

Pick up any newspaper, and you will know we have trouble. Or consider your own life carefully. You can say that "this is the best of all possible worlds" only if you also say that it's the only one possible.

Mankind does need saving. But almost every major argument in the world starts with the questions: "From what?" and "How?" and "What can *I* do?"

We are not going to give you any final answers, either in this book or in the group process that goes with it. We hope you keep on considering the questions and learning answers long after you are through with both the book and the process. Because that's what faith and church and Jesus Christ are all about. It's why we keep on studying the Bible. It's why we keep on hoping in Jesus Christ, in spite of the fact that the news reports never really change.

There is an answer to the questions. That's the Christian faith. It is not easy to say that there is an answer. Many great minds have said there is none.

> *It's all a checker-board of Nights and Days*
> *Where Destiny with Men for Pieces plays:*
> *Hither and thither moves, and mates, and slays,*
> *And one by one back in the Closet lays.*

Rubaiyat of Omar Khayyam, stanza 49

Other great men have said that the only answers are in another life after death.

> Farewell I gladly bid thee,
> False, evil world, farewell.
> Thy life is vain and sinful,
> With thee I would not dwell.

9

I long to be in heaven,
In that untroubled sphere
Where they will be rewarded
Who served their God while here.

The Lutheran Hymnal, No. 407, Valerius Herberger, tr. by Catherine Winkworth

These resources for the process of becoming part of the church give other answers. You will not agree with them all. You will realize that all of them are *church* answers. Many of the answers proposed by men we will ignore. Some of them you will be bringing into the process as your own questions.

Make this book your own. Write into it your questions, whether you have an answer or not. Write into it, now and for many years, your own thinking about the truth of life and God. Use it as a storage place for poems, cartoons, paragraphs which strike you as important to your faith and hope. Turn the book into something that explains *you,* and you will find it useful in your own future crises and joys.

The Editor

Introduction

The last line of the Gospel of John says "There is much else that Jesus did. If it were all to be recorded in detail, I suppose the whole world could not hold the books that would be written." NEB

The world seems to be in the process of being filled with books. Hundreds of thousands of volumes have been written on all aspects of the Christian faith. The challenge then is: what shall be used as a resource for persons in a membership class?

The intent of this volume is to collect some excerpts from the writings of a number of witnesses to the faith, past and present. In this sense its format is similar to the Bible in that we get a glimpse of the witness of many great men in the faith.

In general we have used these guidelines for the material chosen.

1. Excerpts are "bite size" — most of them can be read in a minute or two, and each is sufficiently self-contained to offer some food for thought.
2. The readings contain personal and devotional material in addition to the more usual doctrinal and systematic summaries of the Christian faith.
3. While there are excerpts from quite a number of authors, certain ones are used more frequently. It is hoped that reading the excerpts will whet some appetites for more extensive reading.
4. The readings have been collected under six large categories. Other categories could have been used, but these seem to fit best for this course.

MAN AND HIS PREDICAMENT

● MAN

Did You Ever Fail, Lord?
By *David*

No one pays any attention to me
or what I say, Lord.
I'm nobody, I guess.
I haven't done anything important
or made anything
or won anything.
No one listens when I talk,
no one asks my opinion.
I'm just there
like a window
or a chair.
I tried to build a boat once,
but it fell apart.
I tried to make the baseball team,
but I always threw past third base.
I wrote some articles
for our school paper,
but they didn't want them.
I even tried out for the school play,
but the other kids laughed
when I read my lines.
I seem to fail
at everything.

I don't try anymore
because I'm afraid to fail.
And no one likes to fail
all the time.

If only there was something I could do,
something I could shout about,
something I could make
that was my work,
only mine.
And people would say,
"David did that!"
And my parents would say,
"We're proud of you, son!"

But I can't do anything.
Everyone else is so much better
at everything
than I am.
The more I fail
the more it eats away at me
until I feel weak inside.
I feel like I'm nothing.

Lord,
the world seems full of heroes
and idols and important people.

Where are all the failures?
Where are they hiding?
Where are people like me?
Did you ever fail, Lord?
Did you?
Do you know how I feel?

Do you know what it's like
when everyone looks up at you and says:
"He's a failure."

Norman C. Habel, *For Mature Adults Only,* pp. 28, 29

Addressable

Man is addressable by God. Whether Adam was an individual
or a crowd, this stands out in the scriptural account of creation:
God spoke to Adam and Eve. He did not address the animals or
the stars. Some of the details in Genesis may sound primitive to us,
but we cannot escape this discovery, namely that in some way God
always impinges upon our lives.

Whether this fact was always seen clearly in the past is not our concern now. But few would deny that since man is addressable by God he cannot avoid what is usually described as "confrontation." To live is to be confronted. Our problem then is probably not that we cannot "find God," but that we try to escape confrontation with God.

Responsible

Not only did God address Adam and Eve — he also held them responsible for their words and their actions. As far as we know, he did not approach any other living forms in this way.

Sometimes men have argued about the "how" of man's origin or even arrayed arguments for or against theories of evolution in an attempt to evade this confrontation of responsibility. Darrow and [1] Bryan in their famous encounter might have served men better had they devoted their energy and gifts to assisting others rather than engaging in a fruitless argument and running away from basic issues.

If we are made in "the image of God," it may well be that [2] a major aspect of this is the fact that we are addressable by God and responsible to him. The "search for identity," a genuine problem in our day, may well be a search for God. Man cannot not be man, but in his estrangement he tries to evade the choice of obeying or disobeying God. Man claims that God is a problem to him, but Genesis reminds us that man's problem is that he tries to flee from a God from whom one cannot flee.

Helpless

Christ seemed to be convinced of another truth about man — namely, that man needs help, for Jesus went about doing good — helping, healing, counseling, instructing.

We can use a dozen different metaphors in an attempt to describe this condition of man. Poets may underscore "the tragic view of man," painters may try to depict man's inhumanity to man, counselors cannot escape the fact of man's alienation from man.

The whole emphasis may be somewhat depressing, yet it is realistic. No one, exactly no one — even with the best of efforts —

[1] [Charles Darrow defended a teacher in Tennessee accused of teaching that man evolved from simpler organisms. William Jennings Bryan was counsel for the plaintiff.]

[2] [Genesis 1:27, "God created man in his own image." The words are not explained in Genesis. In some way we are like God.]

always loves everyone or acts consistently from the purest of
motives. Innately, man is a rebel — unlovely, unkind, selfish.

According to Christ, our basic problem is that we ought to love
God and our neighbor as ourselves — yet we cannot respond as we
ought. What is unique in Christ's estimate of man is not that we are
estranged and alienated but that the source of all this rests in our
relationship to God. Adam and Eve insisted on gaining knowledge
that belongs only to God. The Israelites trusted the golden calf
rather than God; they preferred a king to God; they trusted Egypt
and other nations rather than God. An excellent illustration from
the New Testament is the parable of the rich fool, the portrayal of
a man who placed his ultimate loyalty in his material possessions
rather than in God (Luke 12:16-21).

Traditionally this helplessness of man has been traced to the
sin of pride or unbelief. Nothing that man does is free from unbelief
(Romans 3:23) and there is no one exempt from this (Romans 3:10).
We can smooth over this truth or take tranquilizers to forget it, but
that does not remove it. Sometimes it's like a bad dream — you stand
there naked, unable to help yourself.

History and Man

The fourth major disclosure of Jesus about man is encouraging,
for he was convinced that man could change, that he could be
helped, that he could recover from his estrangement and alienation.
The only alternative is total despair.

According to Christ's own statements, this is the major reason
why he came and lived and died and arose: his high estimate of man.
The first hint of this is given early in the history of man (Genesis
3:15). From then on God's approach to man is a long and involved
story, but it is focused on the appearance of Christ. In fact, the
entire cosmos exists to make Bethlehem possible. History and man
now are given meaning and purpose. Not all problems have been
solved, but now man has been given a reason for existence, and
our ultimate purpose is to be truly human.

William D. Streng, *In Search of Ultimates* (Minneapolis, Minn.: Augsburg
Publishing House, 1969), pp. 18, 19, 20.

[3] [In Moses' absence, his brother Aaron made a golden calf as a symbol of God for
the children of Israel. It was treated as an idol, and destroyed by Moses. (Genesis 32)]

[4] [The whole world exists so that God can show His love in the birth of Jesus at
Bethlehem.]

FAUCETS

He will see who he is
and what he is able to do
on land and in the sea.
In the water shortage
and in stagnant water holes
he will explore the world of water.
He will bring life to the city
in the multimillion miles of rivers
walled in
and sent roaring through water mains,
under floors and up high walls,
and over mountains.

He will have dominion over the seas
and the rains,
with his tons of shiny copper pipes
and his cast-iron canals
uniting every corner of every city.
He is able to purify polluted waters,
and to send fresh streams,
cold and clear,
through rusty faucets.
He is able to purify and
to pollute pure deep wells
filtered in sand and rock and time;
city walls can rise and fall
in their water.
He is able to turn cities into deserts,
and dust into city parks.
There is the power of quenched thirst
as his wells and high dams send drink
to the height and breadth of any dwelling place.
At all the faucets and tin drinking cups
they drink in his name.
Drink is still brought to the multitudes,
and the watering of Abraham's camels goes on [5]
in kennels and kitchens.
There are many deep wells
in crowded places,
and lonesome places,
where the Lord serves water
to women from Samaria [6]
and to banquets at weddings.
He will look into the water
and see who he is.

Herbert F. and Mark Brokering, *City and Country*, pp. 56, 57

[5] Rebekah answered the prayer of Abraham's servant by bringing water for his camels, showing she was the one destined to marry Isaac. Genesis 24:10-27

[6] Jesus spoke of God's love to a woman from Samaria, John 4; and provided wine for a marriage banquet in Cana. John 2:1-11

We do not consider it a special honor that we are God's creatures; but because someone is a prince or a great lord, men stare and gape, although the man's office is merely a human creation, as Peter calls it (1 Peter 2:13), and an imitation. For if God had not previously produced His creature and made a man, it would be impossible to make any prince. And yet all men grasp for such an office as if it were a precious and great thing, whereas the fact that I am God's work and creature is much more glorious and great. Therefore menservants, maids, and everybody ought to interest themselves in this high honor and say: I am a human being; this is certainly a higher title than being a prince, for God did not make a prince; men made him. But that I am a human being is the work of God alone.

Ewald M. Plass, *What Luther Says,* Vol. II, p. 877

Even as sin can be looked at in three ways: Rebellion, guilt, or bondage — or maybe, better, in two ways: as an *act* of rebellion resulting in guilt or as a *condition* of bondage — so also man must be seen in contradictory terms. Man is free and responsible but simultaneously helpless and enslaved.

Man *is* evil and man *is* good, and no one-sided evaluation of man that stresses the one pole while ignoring the other is ever going to be complete or accurate! And it is *only* the Bible, among all the diverse systems of human thought, that has the courage and insight and audacity to proclaim that *both* are true, simultaneously, of each of us. The opening chapters of the Bible speak of God's creation and of man within it, and the one word repeated over and over again is "good." "And God saw that it was good." Then he made man ("Let us make man in our image"), and man is good, noble, a creation of God, a reflection of his goodness, so says the Bible. Yet in another place the Bible can turn right around and insist that "the whole world is in the power of the evil one" and that man is a fallen, evil creature, a slave of demonic powers, and we are, all of us, "children of the devil." Behind that poetic imagery of the Bible, behind that metaphorical language which sees man on the one hand made out of the dust of the earth and on the other hand filled with the breath of God, there lies the *only* comprehension of man that is complete and accurate. Man is not good *or* evil, helpless *or* free — he is both! Here the philosophers fail, for they make the part the whole and miss the

point. Only the Bible is comprehensive, for man is both good and
free, both evil and helpless, because sin is both an act and
a condition.

James Kallas, *A Layman's Introduction to Christian Thought,* pp. 28, 32, 33

You are wonderfully made. You are no commoner. You may
have no wealth or hold no office, but you are the Great
Manufacturer's miracle.

You have been outfitted to contain God! That alone makes you
a miracle. Of yourself you are quite insignificant – the sort of
creature who in Shakespeare's words "struts and frets his hour upon
the stage and then is heard no more." Even if you were to corner all
the wealth of the world, your accumulations could not stop the
march of cancer nor stay the microbe's final victory. The paths of
glory lead but to the grave.

But God waits to take up residence within you. He has claimed you as a child; he presses in upon you through the long years. He will not rest until he has invaded your heart and made it his throne. He reshapes you into the sort of creature that can live with him.

Apart from God you are no different from the chemistry of plants or birds. You are a bit more complex than your puppy dog, to be sure, and cannot be satisfied with a bone and a kennel.

Only because you are a candidate for heaven and God's kingdom are you different. Take that away, and you are as common as the grave. But let God in, and you have let all heaven in. The power, the peace, the love, the joy — all heaven's riches become your riches.

We measure men by many standards. Some are rich, some poor; some intelligent, some dull; some beautiful, others plain. God has but one standard: has he been permitted residence within a heart or has he been turned out? If he has been allowed in, he has transformed a man into a miracle!

Alvin Rogness, *Captured by Mystery,* pp. 13, 14

SIN

Sin is a church word that has become so familiar it escapes definition. It may be "breaking the Law of God." It may also be "thinking that you have kept the Law of God." Ordinarily, every definition of sin includes the thought: "what that other person does." Yet the act of judging another man guilty and condemning him belongs under the definition of sin.

It may be necessary for us to decide what is a sin and what is not. Yet that very decision is close to the worst sin: pride. It is much more necessary for us to realize that whatever our definition, we have sinned like every other man, so that we can go on to understand the acts of God for us.

Sin is that which breaks the fellowship with God. The essence of sin can therefore be more closely defined as unbelief. If in faith man is ruled by the loving will of God, the essence of sin consists in that man is not dominated by God, but by something separated from him. This other power is the ego. The essence of sin is, therefore, negatively unbelief and positively egocentricity.

Sin from this point of view is not simply isolated deeds of something imperfect, but a perverse direction of will, which implies a deviation from the essential destiny given to man by God.

Gustaf Aulen, *The Faith of the Christian Church,* pp. 259, 260

The original sin in a man is like his beard, which, though shaved [7] off today so that a man is very smooth around his mouth, yet grows again by tomorrow morning. As long as a man lives, such growth of the hair and the beard does not stop. But when the shovel beats the ground on his grave, it stops. Just so original sin remains in us and bestirs itself as long as we live, but we must resist it and always cut off its hair.

Ewald M. Plass, *What Luther Says,* Vol. III, p. 1302

[7] [The doctrine of original sin says, in effect, that there is not and never has been a truly holy man (except Jesus). Because of what we are, everything any one of us does falls short of perfection.]

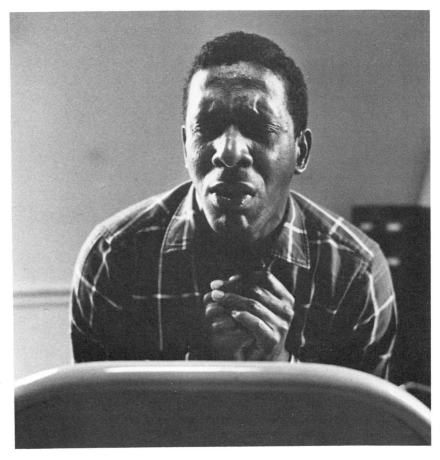

And here is another parable that he told. It was aimed at those who were sure of their own goodness and looked down on everyone else. 'Two men went up to the temple to pray, one a Pharisee and the other a tax-gatherer. The Pharisee stood up and prayed thus: "I thank thee, O God, that I am not like the rest of men, greedy, dishonest, adulterous; or, for that matter, like this tax-gatherer. I fast twice a week; I pay tithes on all that I get." But the other kept his distance and would not even raise his eyes to heaven, but beat upon his breast, saying, "O God, have mercy on me, sinner that I am." It was this man, I tell you, and not the other, who went home acquitted of his sins. For everyone who exalts himself will be humbled; and whoever humbles himself will be exalted.'

Luke 18:9-14 NEB

JUDGMENT

"He'll let us off with fifty years!" one said.
And one, "I always knew that Bible lied!"
One who was philanthropic stood aside,
Patting his sniveling virtues on the head.
"Yes, there may be some—pain," another wheezed.
"One rending touch to fit the soul for bliss."
"A bare formality!" one seemed to hiss.
And everyone was pink and fed and pleased.

Then thunder came, and with an earthquake sound
Shook those fat corpses from their flabby languor.
The sky was furious with immortal anger,
We miserable sinners hugged the ground:
Seeing through all the torment, saying, "Yes,"
God's quiet face, serenely merciless.

Selected Works of Stephen Vincent Benet, p. 411

Let us learn that this is the nature of sin: If God does not soon
remedy the situation and call the sinner back, there is no end to his
flight from God; by trying to excuse his sin with lies he adds sin to
sin until he reaches blasphemy and despair. So one sin always drags
another sin in its train and prepares an eternal ruin until the sinner
finally accuses God Himself rather than acknowledge his sin. Adam
should have said: Lord, I have sinned. But he does not do so; he
accuses God of sin. Adam says in effect: You, Lord, have sinned;
I would have remained holy in Paradise after the bite from the fruit
if only You had remained quiet. That this is the attitude of Adam's
heart and thoughts his words show: I had not taken to flight if Your
voice had not terrified me.

Ewald M. Plass, *What Luther Says,* Vol. III, p. 1309

We poor human beings are blinded and corrupted through sin to
such a degree that we are unable sufficiently to comprehend our
own trouble and defect; otherwise we would guard and protect
ourselves far more carefully against sins. For we observe in
ourselves and other people that we consider sin a very slight hurt
(Schaden), nay, more than that, we love sin and delight in sin.

Ewald M. Plass, *What Luther Says,* Vol. III, p. 1294

The tragedy of man is that reconciliation with his fellow men is always partial, even at best. He needs a forgiveness in the center of his being, and from the heart of the universe. He needs to understand that his offenses against his fellow men, in the final analysis, are a sin against the God who gave life to all men. His estrangement is not merely a break between him and his brothers, nor an estrangement within himself. It is an alienation from him who is God and Savior. Not until he is made whole in God will he know peace and freedom.

Alvin Rogness, *Forgiveness and Confession,* pp. 33, 34

If we claim to be sinless, we are self-deceived and strangers to the truth. If we confess our sins, he is just and may be trusted to forgive our sins and cleanse us from every kind of wrong; but if we say we have committed no sin, we make him out to be a liar, and then his word has no place in us.

1 John 1:8-10 NEB

● LAW

When we try to define law, we have to speak about the purpose of law. Then there is a clear distinction between our human concept of law and the Biblical concept of God's law. Human law describes the evil act in order to differentiate between the transgressor and the obedient. But God's laws describe the human act in order to remove all differences between men.

Man makes laws in order to control evil men. But God makes the Law say No to that, it will not work. We have no hope except in grace, as Jesus showed us.

Now all the words of the law are addressed, as we know, to those who are within the pale of the law, so that no one may have anything to say in self-defence, but the whole world may be exposed to the judgment of God. For (again from Scripture) 'no human being can be justified in the sight of God' for having kept the law: law brings only the consciousness of sin.

But now, quite independently of law, God's justice has been [8] brought to light. The Law and the prophets both bear witness to it: it is God's way of righting wrong, effective through faith in Christ for all who have such faith — all, without distinction. For all alike have sinned, and are deprived of the divine splendour, and all are justified by God's free grace alone, through his act of liberation in the person of Christ Jesus.

Romans 3:19-24 NEB

The Commandments teach and prescribe all sorts of good works, but thereby they are not as yet fulfilled. The Commandments do indeed give directions, but they do not help to carry them out; they teach us what we ought to do, but they give us no strength to do it. Thus they are only designed to make a man see in them his inability to do good and to cause him to learn to despair of himself. This is why they are called the Old Testament and why all of them belong in the Old Testament. For instance, the Commandment: Thou shalt not have evil desires, proves that all of

[8] ["Justice" means that a man gets what he deserves. But before God, who sees all causes and effects, every man deserves exactly alike. So we are "justified" not because we are better than someone else (Law) but because God is gracious, He accepts us all alike (Gospel).]

us are sinners, since no one is able to be without evil desires,
no matter what he does. So he learns to despair of himself, to
seek help elsewhere in order to be without evil desires and thus to
fulfill by Another the Commandment which he is unable to keep by
himself. In like manner, it is impossible for us to keep any of the
other Commandments.

Ewald M. Plass, *What Luther Says,* Vol. II, p. 762

Paul, the leading interpreter of Christianity during the New
Testament period, led Christianity in its earliest battle — that against
legalism. Every religion, including the Christian, tends to become
legalistic. That is, it teaches that man must obey certain rules and
regulations to win the favor and rewards of God.

Both Jesus and Paul fought against legalism. Jesus asserted that
when a man had done everything that he could, he still was to count
himself an unprofitable servant (Luke 17:10). That is, he was not to
suppose that he had earned some kind of payment from God.
Similarly, Jesus taught that God makes his rain to fall on the just
and on the unjust (Matt. 5:45). God does not place an umbrella
over the heads of those who are good so that they have a special
protection from the slings and arrows of outrageous fortune. The
slowness with which Christians have come to accept this basic fact
in Jesus' teaching is strange. It still seems natural for many to
suppose that a life of superior goodness will receive a superior
reward if not here, then surely hereafter. Jesus, however, explicitly
denies this in his parable of the Laborers in the Vineyard (Matt.
20:1-16). The men who have worked from the dew of early morn
and through the noontide heat do not receive any more pay at the
end of the day than the men who worked but an hour.

The early Christians, led by Paul, came to see that legalism, the
attempt to earn rewards from God by obeying certain rules, is
basically wrong. It is wrong because it commercializes religion.
One is good because he expects to get paid for his good deeds.
It is wrong because it leads so easily to pride and hypocrisy, as we
see in the Pharisees. Because the Pharisee keeps the law a little [9]

[9] [The Pharisees were a religious and political party in Israel who insisted that the
Jews were called to keep the laws of God faithfully. They were sincere, dedicated,
and good people; but their teachings did tend to conceal the fact that God is gracious.]

better than others, he feels far superior. Furthermore, he is
continually tempted into the hypocrisy of believing that he is doing
better than he really is. On the other hand, men like Paul found
that legalism led to despair. As they realized how far short they
were falling of the ideal goodness, they despaired of themselves,
their salvation, and their reward.

William E. Hordern, *A Layman's Guide,* pp. 5-7

The Law and Commandment of God indeed give me the right
direction; they show me life, righteousness, and eternal life, preach
and tell me much about these. The Law is a message directing me to
life; and this teaching should and must be preserved. But the Law
does not give me life. A hand that points out the way to me is
a useful member of the body. But if I have no feet, nor wagon to
ride in, and no horses to mount, I shall surely not travel along the
way. The hand will not take me on the way, yet it correctly shows
me the way. Just so the Law serves the purpose of indicating the
will of God and of convincing us that we are unable to keep it; for
it shows us what a man is and what he is able and unable to do.
Moreover, the Law has been given us in order to reveal sin; but it
cannot help us from sins, nor can it pull us out of them. It shows
us a mirror into which we are to look and become aware that we do
not have righteousness and life. Then begins the cry: Oh, come,
Lord Jesus Christ, help us, and grant us grace that we may be able
to do what the Law requires of us.

Ewald M. Plass, *What Luther Says,* Vol. II, p. 762

I'm at the end of my rope, Lord.
I am shattered,
I am broken.
Since this morning I have been struggling to escape temptation,
    which, now wary, now persuasive, now tender, now sensuous,
    dances before me like a seductive girl at a fair.
I don't know what to do.
I don't know where to go.
It spies on me, follows me, engulfs me.
When I leave a room I find it seated and waiting for me in the next.
When I seize a newspaper, there it is, hidden in the words of some
    innocuous article.

I go out, and see it smiling at me on an unknown face.

I turn away and look at the wall, and it leaps at me from a poster.

I return to work, to find it dozing on my files, and when I gather
my papers, it wakes up.

In despair, I take my poor head in my hands, I shut my eyes, to
see nothing,

But I discover that it is more lively than ever, comfortably settled
within me.

For it has broken my door open, it has slipped into my body,
my veins,
to the very tips of my fingers.

It has seeped into the crevices of my memory

And sings into the ear of my imagination.

It plays on my nerves as on the strings of a guitar.

I no longer know where I stand, Lord.

I no longer know whether or not I want this sin that beckons to
me.

I no longer know whether I pursue it or am pursued.

I am dizzy, and the void draws me the way a chasm draws the rash
mountaineer who can no longer either advance or retreat.

Lord, Lord, help me.

Michael Quoist, *Prayers,* pp. 132, 133

Personal Testimonies from the Bible

> I am wearied with groaning;
> all night long my pillow is wet with tears,
> I soak my bed with weeping.
> Grief dims my eyes;
>> they are worn out with all my woes.

Psalm 6:6, 7, NEB

> When I look up at thy heavens, the work of thy fingers,
>> the moon and the stars set in their place by thee,
> what is man that thou shouldst remember him,
>> mortal man that thou shouldst care for him?
> Yet thou hast made him little less than a god,
> crowning him with glory and honour.
> Thou makest him master over all thy creatures;
> thou hast put everything under his feet:
> all sheep and oxen, all the wild beasts,
>> the birds in the air and the fish in the sea,
>> and all that moves along the paths of ocean.

Psalm 8:3-8, NEB

> Wash away all my guilt
>> and cleanse me from my sin.
> For well I know my misdeeds,
> and my sins confront me all the day long.
> Against thee, thee only, I have sinned
> and done what displeases thee,
> so that thou mayest be proved right in thy charge
>> and just in passing sentence.

Psalm 51:2-4, NEB

> I have seen violence and strife in the city;
>> day and night they encircle it,
>>> all along its walls;
>> it is filled with trouble and mischief,
>>> alive with rumour and scandal,
>> and its public square is never free
>>> from violence and spite.

It was no enemy that taunted me,
    or I should have avoided him;
no adversary that treated me with scorn,
    or I should have kept out of his way.
It was you, a man of my own sort,
    my comrade, my own dear friend,
with whom I kept pleasant company
    in the house of God.

Psalm 55:9-15, NEB

Then I turned and gave myself up to despair, reflecting upon all my labour and toil here under the sun. For anyone who toils with wisdom, knowledge, and skill must leave it all to a man who has spent no labour on it. This too is emptiness and utterly wrong. What reward has a man for all his labour, his scheming, and his toil here under the sun? All his life long his business is pain and vexation to him; even at night his mind knows no rest. This too is emptiness. There is nothing better for a man to do than to eat and drink and enjoy himself in return for his labours.

Ecclesiastes 2:20-24, NEB

I do not even acknowledge my own actions as mine, for what I do is not what I want to do, but what I detest. But if what I do is against my will, it means that I agree with the law and hold it to be admirable. But as things are, it is no longer I who perform the action, but sin that lodges in me. For I know that nothing good lodges in me — in my unspiritual nature, I mean — for though the will to do good is there, the deed is not. The good which I want to do, I fail to do; but what I do is the wrong which is against my will; and if what I do is against my will, clearly it is no longer I who am the agent, but sin that has its lodging in me.

Romans 7:15-20, NEB

JESUS CHRIST: THE WORD OF GRACE

The Good News of Jesus Christ is so rich in meaning that many key words have been used to describe it — Gospel, justification, redemption, atonement, etc. They are like many facets on a diamond each giving a different perspective and each reflecting some of the brilliance which is our Lord.

In this unit, we will gather our reading under seven headings. We recognize that some important headings have been left out (in the interest of brevity) but we believe there are enough to give a glimpse of Jesus Christ: The Word of Grace.

His life is summarized later in this book. Whatever we say or think of Jesus Christ, we begin with the fact that He was a man who lived and died and rose again in the early days of the Roman empire, in the tiny land of Palestine. He is not a myth. Whatever He means to us is real, it starts with a history.

His life and death and resurrection convinced His disciples and us that He is God incarnate, the Word of God, our Lord. That means that we who follow Jesus see God in Him. He is the way we know God. Our God is what Jesus was. And if our God is like that, then our blessed and good life is also like what Jesus was.

This evil is planted in all human hearts by nature: If God were willing to sell His grace, we would accept it more quickly and gladly than when He offers it for nothing.

Ewald M. Plass, *What Luther Says*, Vol. II, p. 604

● CHRIST

Have this mind among yourselves, which you have in Christ Jesus, who, though he was in the form of God, did not count equality with God a thing to be grasped, but emptied himself, taking the form

of a servant, being born in the likeness of men. And being found
in human form he humbled himself and became obedient unto death,
even death on a cross. Therefore God has highly exalted him and
bestowed on him the name which is above every name, that at the
name of Jesus every knee should bow, in heaven and on earth, and
every tongue confess that Jesus Christ is Lord, to the glory of God
the Father.

Philippians 2:5-11, RSV

I believe that Jesus Christ—
true God, Son of the Father
    from eternity,
and true man, born of the Virgin Mary—
is my Lord.

At great cost
He has saved and redeemed me,
a lost and condemned person,
He has freed me
from sin, death,
and the power of the devil—
not with silver or gold,
but with His holy and precious blood
and His innocent suffering and death.

All this He has done that I may be His own,
live under Him in His kingdom,
and serve Him in everlasting righteousness,
    innocence, and blessedness,
just as He is risen from the dead
    and lives and rules eternally.
This is most certainly true.

Martin Luther, The Small Catechism in Contemporary English

He puts a Babe in a crib. Our common sense revolts and says, "Could not God have saved the world some other way?" I would not have sent an angel. I would simply have called in the devil and said, "Let my people go." The Christian faith is foolishness. It says that God can do anything and yet makes him so weak that either his Son had no power and wisdom or else the whole story is made up. Surely the God who in the beginning said: "Let there be light," "Let there be a firmament," "Let the dry land appear," could have said to the devil, "Give me back my people, my Christians." God does not even send an angel to take the devil by the nose. He sends, as it were, an earthworm lying in weakness, helpless without his mother, and he suffers him to be nailed to a cross. The devil says, "I will judge him." So spoke Caiaphas and Pilate, "He is nothing but a carpenter," and then in his weakness and infirmity he crunches the devil's back and alters the whole world. He suffered himself to be trodden under the foot of man and to be crucified, and through weakness he takes the power and the Kingdom.

Roland H. Bainton, *The Martin Luther Christmas Book,* pp. 47, 48

Here is a man who was born in an obscure village, the child of a peasant woman. He grew up in another obscure village. He worked in a carpenter shop until He was thirty, and then for three years He was an itinerant preacher. He never wrote a book. He never held an office.

He never owned a home. He never set foot inside a big city. He never traveled two hundred miles from the place where He was born. He had no credentials but Himself.

He had nothing to do with this world except the naked power of His divine manhood. While still a young man, the tide of popular opinion turned against Him. His friends ran away. One of them denied Him. He was turned over to His enemies. He went through the mockery of a trial. He was nailed upon a cross between two thieves.

His executioners gambled for the only piece of property He had on earth while He was dying — and that was His coat. When He was dead He was taken down and laid in a borrowed grave through the pity of a friend.

Nineteen wide centuries have come and gone and today He is the centerpiece of the human race and the leader of progress. I am far within the mark when I say that all the armies that ever marched, and all the navies that ever were built, and all the parliaments that ever sat, and all the kings that ever reigned, put together have not affected the life of man upon this earth as powerfully as that One Solitary Life.

"One Solitary Life," author unknown

Gerald H. Kennedy, *A Reader's Notebook*, p. 147

I'm trying here to prevent anyone from saying the really silly thing that people often say about Him: "I'm ready to accept Jesus as a great moral teacher, but I don't accept His claim to be God." That's the one thing we mustn't say. A man who was merely a man and said the sort of things Jesus said wouldn't be a great moral teacher. He'd either be a lunatic—on a level with the man who says he's a poached egg—or else he'd be the Devil of Hell. You must make your choice. Either this man was, and is, the Son of God: or else a madman or something worse. You can shut Him up for a fool, you can spit at Him and kill Him as a demon; or you can fall at His feet and call Him Lord and God. But don't let us come with any patronising nonsense about His being a great human teacher. He hasn't left that open to us. He didn't intend to.

We are faced, then, with a frightening alternative. This man we're talking about either was (and is) just what He said or else a lunatic, or something worse. Now it seems to me obvious that He wasn't either a lunatic or a fiend: and consequently, however strange or terrifying or unlikely it may seem, I have to accept the view that He was and is God. God has landed on this enemy-occupied world in human form.

C. S. Lewis, *The Case for Christianity,* p. 45

In the midst of dense places
and thick forests
there is a burst of new life.
A new tree grows.
Jesus grew in wisdom and in stature
and in favor with God and man.
In the midst of dense customs
and thick traditions and large habits and deep roots,
there was the burst of a new day. A new Man,
in the middle of old customs and habits and traditions.
Out of the lineage of David
and in the womb of a Jewish maiden
a Savior had come into life.
Bringing rest to the weary traveler.
A refuge for those in flight.
Comfort for heavy laden.
This new tree will stand
at the end of all seasons and all time.
Men, women, and children shall feast from his fruit
and so live for ever and ever.
The stem of Jesse did grow in the midst [1]
of density and destruction,
and has been named the Tree of Life.

Herbert F. Brokering and Sister Noemi, *In Due Season*, Spring

[1] ["The stem of Jesse" refers to Isaiah 11:1 (KJV). Jesse was the father of David. The passage states that a descendant of David would bring peace and salvation to man. It is fulfilled in Jesus.]

● *Atonement*

*To "atone" means to make amends, to do something that
cancels out a wrong. That is what Jesus did, and He did it for us.
But what He did and how He did it are much more than we can
imagine, and we cannot insist that every Christian should be limited
to what we can say. The readings list some of the many ways people
have described His work. The mystery remains for you to think and
talk about.*

For twenty centuries the Church has been proclaiming salvation,
and the grace and forgiveness of God, to a humanity oppressed with
guilt. How then is it that even amongst the most fervent believers
there are so few free, joyous, confident souls?

It seems to me that this arises, at least to a large extent, from
a psychological attitude which I now want to stress, namely, the idea
deeply engraved in the heart of all men, that everything must be
paid for. . . .

But the wonderful announcement of God's free grace, which
effaces guilt, runs up against the intuition which every man has, that
a price must be paid. The reply which comes is the supreme message
of the Bible, its supreme revelation; it is God Himself who pays,
God Himself has paid the price once for all, and the most costly that
could be paid—His own death, in Jesus Christ, on the Cross. The
obliteration of our guilt is free for us because God has paid the
price.

Paul Tournier, *Guilt and Grace*, pp. 174, 185

In contrast to other religions, Christianity has a unique point of
view. Whereas most religions believe that man has to do something
to atone to God, Christianity teaches that God himself has performed
the atoning work. Other religions perform sacrifices in order that God
might turn his angry face back toward man and forgive him.
Christianity teaches that God has performed a sacrifice, in and
through Jesus, which has brought God and man back into fellowship
with each other. But the problem arises: What did God do? Paul
is clear that Jesus' death was central, but he gives no clear explanation.
The Church never held a council on this doctrine, as it did on the
Trinity and the nature of Christ. No one doctrine has been held

from the beginning, and hence it is difficult to speak of the orthodox [2]
position.

The so-called classical doctrine of atonement was accepted for
more than a thousand years. According to this, Satan had gained
the souls of men because they had sinned. But God made a bargain
with Satan: He would give Satan the soul of Jesus, even though
Satan did not deserve him, if Satan would release the souls of men
who accepted Jesus. Satan agreed, thinking that Jesus was only
a good man. But when he received Jesus, he found that he could not
hold him for he was the Son of God. And so Satan ended up with
neither the souls of those who accepted Christ nor Christ himself.
This doctrine sounds crude and seems to implicate God in a rather
shady trick upon the Devil. It has, none the less, two profound
thoughts. It expresses faith that in the death and resurrection of
Jesus, God has conquered the forces of evil. Good is more powerful
than evil. In the second place, it points to the fact that evil tends
to overreach and thus destroy itself. "Give a man enough rope and
he will hang himself." This is a fact of life. If Hitler, for example,
had been content with a little less he might still rule Germany. Evil
cannot be satisfied, and in its insatiable greed it brings destruction
upon itself. But despite these insights, the doctrine seemed too
crude, and in the eleventh century two new doctrines were put
forward.

The first came from Anselm. He argued that man owed obedience
to God, the ruler of the universe, but he had failed to obey and
hence he fell into debt to God. He had dishonored God. Justice
demanded either that the debt be paid to God or that man be
punished. Either way would uphold God's prestige as the moral
ruler of man. But God did not want to punish man eternally, for his
purpose in creating man was to have fellowship with him. Man
could not give God satisfaction since man already owed perfect
obedience and could do no more. If God waved the sin aside and
simply forgave, his honor and prestige as the ruler would be called
into question. We have a dilemma; man owed the debt, but only
God could pay it. So, God sent Jesus, who was both God and man.
Because he was God, he could pay the debt; because he was also
man he could pay it for man. But even Jesus could not pay it by
living a perfect life, for, as man, he already owed that to God. But
Jesus did not deserve to die since he had not sinned. Consequently,

[2] ["Orthodox" means "the true teaching." In a historic statement like this, it means
a teaching that is generally accepted by all true Christians.]

when Jesus gave himself over to death, he paid the debt for man. God's honor was vindicated so that he could forgive those who came to him through Christ.

This theory did not express perfectly what the Church wanted to say and it was never accepted officially. It made God sound very much like a feudal lord who was afraid his serfs might get out of hand if he appeared too lenient. Yet it did express the Church's belief that forgiveness is not something simple or easy. It costs God to forgive.

Abelard presented another theory. He insisted that there was nothing on God's side that made forgiveness impossible. But forgiveness is a two-way affair. You cannot forgive a man who does not wish to be forgiven. Forgiveness means the restoration of broken fellowship; but one cannot restore the fellowship if the other does not wish it restored. This, says Abelard, was God's problem. He wanted to forgive man, but man went his merry way sinning and did not repent or ask forgiveness. So God acted; he sent his Son to suffer and die for man as a manifestation of God's great love. When man sees this he is moved to shame and repents so that God is able to forgive him.

Abelard's doctrine also says something that orthodox Christianity wanted to say. In the death of Christ we see the love of God in such a way that we are moved to repent. None the less, Abelard's doctrine won him the charge of heresy. The orthodox argument against it usually goes like this: If a man jumps into the water and saves me while I am drowning, the act reveals his love. But if we are walking along the beach and he suddenly says, "See how much I love you," and then jumps into the water and drowns, we are inclined to think the sun got too hot for him. In other words, Christ's death can only be a revelation of God's love for man if it was a necessary sacrifice. It is meaningless if man could be saved without it.

Orthodox Christianity, while it was not completely satisfied with Anselm, usually has taken some form of his theory. Christ, it has believed, was in some sense our substitute; he died to pay our debt or he suffered the punishment that we ought to have suffered for our sin. Protestant orthodoxy was inclined to put the doctrine in terms of the law courts. Man had committed crimes for which he must be punished, but Jesus "took the rap" in man's place. So interpreted, the doctrine has the effect of Abelard's; it wins man to repent, but it does so because the sacrifice was a necessary one and not a grand gesture.

This is the main outline of the orthodox position in theology
upon which Christians from widely separated denominations would
agree. It is this body of thought, with a few implications that we
shall see as we go along, that we have in mind when we speak of
orthodox Christianity.

William E. Hordern, *A Layman's Guide to Protestant Theology,* pp. 25-28,
1968 ed.

Behold, my servant shall prosper,
he shall be lifted up, exalted to the heights.

Time was when many were aghast at you, my people;
so now many nations recoil at sight of him,
and kings curl their lips in disgust.
For they see what they had never been told
    and things unheard before fill their thoughts.

Who could have believed what we have heard,
and to whom has the power of the Lord been revealed?

He grew up before the Lord like a young plant
    whose roots are in parched ground;
he had no beauty, no majesty to draw our eyes,
    no grace to make us delight in him;
his form, disfigured, lost all the likeness of a man,
    his beauty changed beyond human semblance.
    He was despised, he shrank from the sight of men,
        tormented and humbled by suffering;
        we despised him, we held him of no account,
        a thing from which men turn away their eyes.
Yet on himself he bore our sufferings,
        our torments he endured,
    while we counted him smitten by God,
        struck down by disease and misery;
    but he was pierced for our transgressions,
        tortured for our iniquities;
    the chastisement he bore is health for us
        and by his scourging we are healed.
    We had all strayed like sheep,
    each of us had gone his own way;
    but the Lord laid upon him
        the guilt of us all.

Isaiah 52:13 – 53:6 NEB

Therefore, now that we have been justified through faith, let us continue at peace with God through our Lord Jesus Christ, through whom we have been allowed to enter the sphere of God's grace, where we now stand. Let us exult in the hope of the divine splendour that is to be ours. More than this: let us even exult in our present sufferings, because we know that suffering trains us to endure, and endurance brings proof that we have stood the test, and this proof is the ground of hope. Such a hope is no mockery, because God's love has flooded our inmost heart through the Holy Spirit he has given us.

For at the very time when we were still powerless, then Christ died for the wicked. Even for a just man one of us would hardly die, though perhaps for a good man one might actually brave death; but Christ died for us while we were yet sinners, and that is God's own proof of his love towards us. And so, since we have now been justified by Christ's sacrificial death, we shall all the more certainly be saved through him from final retribution. For if, when we were God's enemies, we were reconciled to him through the death of his Son, how much more, now that we are reconciled, shall we be saved by his life! But that is not all: we also exult in God through our Lord Jesus, through whom we have now been granted reconciliation.

Romans 5:1-11 NEB

For the love of Christ leaves us no choice, when once we have reached the conclusion that one man died for all and therefore all mankind has died. His purpose in dying for all was that men, while still in life, should cease to live for themselves, and should live for him who for their sake died and was raised to life. With us therefore worldly standards have ceased to count in our estimate of any man; even if once they counted in our understanding of Christ, they do so now no longer. When anyone is united to Christ, there is a new world; the old order has gone, and a new order has already begun.

From first to last this has been the work of God. He has reconciled us men to himself through Christ, and he has enlisted us in this service of reconciliation. What I mean is, that God was in Christ reconciling the world to himself, no longer holding men's misdeeds against them, and that he has entrusted us with the message of reconciliation. We come therefore as Christ's ambassadors. It is as if God were appealing to you through us: in Christ's name, we implore you, be reconciled to God! Christ was innocent of sin, and yet for our sake God made him one with the sinfulness of men, so that in him we might be made one with the goodness of God himself. Sharing in God's work, we urge this appeal upon you: you have received the grace of God; do not let it go for nothing. God's own words are:

> 'In the hour of my favour I gave heed to you;
> on the day of deliverance I came to your aid.'

The hour of favour has now come; now, I say, has the day of deliverance dawned.

---

2 Corinthians 5:14—6:2 NEB

For through faith you are all sons of God in union with Christ Jesus. Baptized into union with him, you have all put on Christ as a garment. There is no such thing as Jew and Greek, slave and freeman, male and female; for you are all one person in Christ Jesus. But if you thus belong to Christ, you are the 'issue' of Abraham, and so heirs by promise.

This is what I mean: so long as the heir is a minor, he is no better off than a slave, even though the whole estate is his; he is under guardians and trustees until the date fixed by his father. And so it was with us. During our minority we were slaves to the elemental spirits of the universe, but when the term was completed, God sent his own Son, born of a woman, born under the law, to purchase freedom for the subjects of the law, in order that we might attain the status of sons.

To prove that you are sons, God has sent into our hearts the Spirit of his Son, crying 'Abba! Father!' You are therefore no longer a slave but a son, and if a son, then also by God's own act an heir.

Formerly, when you did not acknowledge God, you were the slaves of beings which in their nature are no gods. But now that you do acknowledge God – or rather, now that he has acknowledged you – how can you turn back to the mean and beggarly spirits of the elements? Why do you propose to enter their service all over again? You keep special days and months and seasons and years. You make me fear that all the pains I spent on you may prove to be labour lost.

Galatians 3:26 – 4:11 NEB

● GRACE

Grace is how God acts toward us: in unconditional love. But He is not our God unless we follow His principle of action, in grace toward one another. "Justified by grace" means our excuse for being is that God loves us. We have no other. "Saved by grace" means also that only unconditional love between us will enable man to live with man. We need to know that "Jesus loves me." We also need to know that Jesus loves him — the other man, every other man.

A good song may well be sung often. Grace consists in this, that God is merciful to us, shows Himself gracious for the sake of the

Lord Christ, forgives all sins, and will not impute them unto us for [3]
eternal death. This is grace: the forgiveness of sins for the sake of
the Lord Christ, the covering up of all sins.

Ewald M. Plass, *What Luther Says,* Vol. II, p. 603.

Cheap grace is the deadly enemy of our Church. We are fighting
to-day for costly grace. . . .

Cheap grace means grace as a doctrine, a principle, a system. It
means forgiveness of sins proclaimed as a general truth, the love of
God taught as the Christian "conception" of God. An intellectual
assent to that idea is held to be of itself sufficient to secure remission
of sins. The Church which holds the correct doctrine of grace has, it
is supposed, *ipso facto* a part in that grace. In such a Church the
world finds a cheap covering for its sins; no contrition is required, [4]
still less any real desire to be delivered from sin. Cheap grace
therefore amounts to a denial of the living Word of God, in fact, a
denial of the Incarnation of the Word of God. Cheap grace means
the justification of sin without the justification of the sinner. . . .

Cheap grace is the preaching of forgiveness without requiring
repentance, baptism without church discipline, Communion without
confession, absolution without personal confession. Cheap grace is
grace without discipleship, grace without the cross, grace without
Jesus Christ, living and incarnate . . . .

Costly grace is the gospel which must be *sought* again and
again, the gift which must be *asked* for, the door at which a man must
knock.

Such grace is *costly* because it calls us to follow, and it is *grace*
because it calls us to follow *Jesus Christ.* . . . It is costly because
it condemns sins, and grace because it justifies the sinner. Above all
it is *costly* because it cost God the life of his Son: "ye were bought
at a price," and what has cost God much cannot be cheap for us.
Above all, it is *grace* because God did not reckon his Son too dear
a price to pay for our life, but delivered him up for us. Costly grace
is the Incarnation of God.

Dietrich Bonhoeffer, *The Cost of Discipleship,* pp. 45, 46, 47, 48

Man receives grace at once and fully. Thus he is saved. Good
works do not need to come to his assistance but are to follow. It is

[3] ["Impute" means "charge them to."]

[4] ["Contrition" means being really sorry, enough to change your ways and resolve
never to repeat the error.]

precisely as if God were to produce a fresh, green tree out of a dry
log, which tree would then bear its natural fruit.

A very great, strong, mighty, and active matter is this grace of
God. It does not lie asleep in the soul, as visionary preachers fable;
nor does it let itself be carried about, as a painted board carries its
color. No, none of that! Grace hears, it leads, it drives, it draws,
it changes, it works all in man, and lets itself be distinctly felt and
experienced. It is hidden, but its works are evident. Words and works
show where it dwells, just as the fruit and the leaves of a tree
indicate the kind and the character of the tree.

Ewald M. Plass, *What Luther Says,* Vol. II, p. 613

● FAITH

*We are saved by grace through faith. Faith is how grace takes
hold on us and moves us. For faith, you need to know about Jesus.
You have to agree that He is right and true. And you have to trust
Him—put your future and your hope in His hands of love, not in
your own efforts.*

*But faith is more than that. It's staking your life, your ambition,
and your fear on the belief that He is the Way for you, that His
love will work in your life, that grace is the most blessed way for
you to live. Faith is taking the risk in all that you do that Jesus is
what you believe Him to be in words: your Lord and Savior.*

No work is so evil that it can damn a man, and no work is so
good that it can save a man; but faith alone saves us, and unbelief
damns us. The fact that someone falls into adultery does not damn
him. Rather the adultery indicates that he has fallen from faith.
This damns him; otherwise adultery would be impossible for him.
So, then, nothing makes a good tree except faith. For this is what
the Lord says (Luke 3:9): The tree should be cut down. He does
not say that the fruits are to be knocked off. This is why works of
love do not make me good: but faith alone does, faith in which I do
these works and bear this fruit. This is the reason why we must
begin with faith.

Ewald M. Plass, *What Luther Says,* Vol. I, p. 475

But I could think that in the figure of Jesus we saw Immanuel,
that is, God, that is, Love. It was a figure who, appearing so

inauspiciously among us, broke up our secularist and our religious categories, and beckoned us and judged us and damned us and saved us, and exhibited to us a kind of life that participates in the indestructible. And it was a figure who announced the validity of our eternal effort to discover significance and beauty beyond inanition and horror by announcing to us the unthinkable: redemption.

It was a figure we could neither own nor manage. We claimed it as our special possession, and exacted tribute and built shrines and established forms in which to incarcerate it, only to discover that it had fled. It would not be enshrined. It was the figure of a man, and a man must live and walk with other men or die, and this man was alive. He scorned our scruple to shelter him and to prop up his doctrine. What he spoke, he spoke loudly and freely, and his words were their own defense. When we tried to help things by urging sweetness and light, or by interdicting what looked threatening, or by tithing mint, anise, and cumin, or by devising rituals and nonrituals, we found him towering above us, scorching our efforts into clinkers, and recalling us to wildness and risk and humility and love. Just at the moment when we thought we had guaranteed our own standing in his good favor by organizing an airtight doctrine or a flawless liturgy or an unassailable morality, he escaped us, and returned with his hammer to demolish things. Try as we might, we could not own him. We could not protect him. We could not incarcerate him. For he always emerged as our judge, exposing our cynicism and fright by the candor and boldness of his love. He tore our secularist schemes to ribbons by announcing doom and our religious schemes to tatters by announcing love. . . .

We experienced this announcement as both death-dealing and life-giving. It was death-dealing because we knew our own incorrigible cupidity — the energy that makes us shriek for the shovel in the sandbox, cut into the ticket line, rush for the subway seat, display our prowess, parade our clothes, and pursue delights regardless of prior considerations. . . .

But I show you a different way. It is an alien and a frightening one. It is called Love. It asks that you forswear your busy effort to collect the bits of bliss and novelty that lie about. It asks that you disavow your attempt to enlarge your own identity by diminishing that of others. It asks that you cease your effort to safeguard your own claim to well-being by assuming the inferiority of others' claims.

5 ["Mint, anise, and cumin" were minor crops. Tithing them (giving 10%) means being frantically meticulous about obeying the law to be "good." See Matthew 23:23.]

It asks, actually, that you die. . . .

So there is this, I thought, as an alternative to despair. At least it is not meliorism or optimism. But the *peril* of staking everything on this kind of vision . . . Incarnation. Redemption. These are far from verifiable, and this is ridiculous in an age that insists on verification.

And *caritas*. This is impossible. How is a man to opt for a kind [6] of life in which he stands to lose everything? I mean, if you want to get a seat on the subway you have to push for it. *Tant pis* for the one [7] who has to stand. And if you want the ecstasies, you have to go flat out to accumulate them. How can a man be expected to opt out of everything that looks important on the chance that there is more to it all than meets the eye? It is too great a risk.

Perhaps that is what is asked, I thought. Perhaps there is no escape from risk. Perhaps there is no explanation offered for the staggering ambiguities, nor any answer given to the agonizing questions. Perhaps a man is asked to opt with all his might for authenticity. Perhaps the great thing is to respond, with as much integrity as he can summon, to the cues. There *are* some — in his own consciousness, in his art, in his world. And there is this great light that has appeared in the murk, like a morning star. It is there, silent and glorious. An odd road marker. But perhaps a man is asked to go that way on the supposition that it is not all a ghastly cheat.

Yes. Perhaps that is what is asked.

Thomas Howard, *Christ the Tiger,* pp. 154 – 156, 159 – 160

God could easily become rich if He properly looked out for Himself and denied us the use of His creatures. If at one time He were to keep the sun from shining, at another lock up the supply of air, and yet again hold up the supply of water and extinguish the fire, we should be glad to expend all our money for these blessings. But because they are given to us so profusely, we want them as our just due. We dare anyone to deny us these things! Therefore the lavishness of God's benefactions actually makes us think faith less important.

Ewald M. Plass, *What Luther Says,* Vol. I, p. 483

[6] ["Caritas" means love — the kind of love that abandons all self-interest.]

[7] [*Tant pis* — French for "too bad."]

A person may carry a hundred gulden wrapped in paper, or he may transport them in an iron chest; yet the treasure is entirely the same. Though you or I have a stronger or weaker faith in Christ, Christ is, after all, the same, and we have everything in Him, whether we have grasped it with a strong or with a weak faith. All service of God consists in this: Believe in Christ, whom the Father has sent; accept whatever He will preach to you. You can do nothing in heaven or on earth that is more pleasing to God than that is.

Ewald M. Plass, *What Luther Says,* Vol. I, p. 488

● *FORGIVENESS*

Forgiveness seems a simple word, until you ask who, how, and why? You can forgive only a sinner. There are no conditions to be met first, or it is not forgiveness. And forgiveness is the way to call someone out of sin—hate, envy, coveting, lying, or stealing.

"God forgives" means that forgiveness is God's way of dealing with the problem of our evil. It is the effective way to stop evil. Anything else only multiplies it. When we accept, or receive, forgiveness it means we agree that forgiving is the way we will deal with sin. There are no conditions. There are only the spreading results of forgiving and being forgiven.

If the great, sublime article called the forgiveness of sins is correctly understood, it makes one a genuine Christian and gives one eternal life. This is the very reason why it must be taught in Christendom with unflagging diligence and without ceasing, so that people may learn to understand it plainly.

Ewald M. Plass, *What Luther Says,* Vol. I, p. 514

The article of the forgiveness of sins is the most important . . . and it is of all the most comforting. To Satan it is truly the worst, and it is the most hateful. This is the reason why Paul always has on his tongue: grace, grace, grace! He does this to spite the devil.

Ewald M. Plass, *What Luther Says,* Vol. I, p. 515

When God, through His grace, grants us forgiveness of sins without our merit, so that we need not purchase it or earn it ourselves, we are at once inclined to draw this reassuring conclusion and to say: Well, so we need no longer do good! — Therefore, in addition to teaching the doctrine of faith in His grace, God must constantly combat this notion and show that this is not at all His meaning. Sins are assuredly not forgiven in order that they should be committed, but in order that they should stop; otherwise it should more justly be called the *per*mission of sins, not the *re*mission of sins.

Ewald M. Plass, *What Luther Says,* Vol. I, p. 520

"Confess your faults one to another" (James 5:16) He who is alone with his sin is utterly alone. It may be that Christians, notwithstanding corporate worship, common prayer, and all their fellowship in service, may still be left to their loneliness. The final break-through to fellowship does not occur, because, though they have fellowship with one another as believers and as devout people, they do not have fellowship as the undevout, as sinners. The pious fellowship permits no one to be a sinner. So everybody must conceal his sin from himself and from the fellowship. We dare not be sinners. Many Christians are unthinkably horrified when a real sinner is suddenly discovered among the righteous. So we remain alone with our sin, living in lies and hypocrisy. The fact is that we *are* sinners!

But it is the grace of the Gospel, which is so hard for the pious to understand, that it confronts us with the truth and says: You are a sinner, a great, desperate sinner; now come, as the sinner that you are, to God who loves you. He wants you as you are; He does not want anything from you, a sacrifice, a work; He wants you alone. "My son, give me thine heart" (Prov. 23:26). God has come to you to save the sinner. Be glad! This message is liberation through truth. You can hide nothing from God. The mask you wear before men will do you no good before Him. He wants to see you as you are, He wants to be gracious to you. You do not have to go on lying to yourself and your brothers, as if you were without sin; you can dare to be a sinner. Thank God for that; He loves the sinner but He hates sin.

Dietrich Bonhoeffer, *Life Together,* pp. 110, 111

This is how you should pray:
"Our Father in heaven,
Thy name be hallowed;
Thy kingdom come,
Thy will be done,
On earth as in heaven.
Give us today our daily bread.
Forgive us the wrong we have done,
As we have forgiven those who have wronged us.
And do not bring us to the test,
But save us from the evil one."

For if you forgive others the wrongs they have done, your heavenly Father will also forgive you; but if you do not forgive others, then the wrongs you have done will not be forgiven by your Father.

Matthew 6:9-15 NEB

● SALVATION

We are saved by grace through faith. Salvation is what we are saved into. What we are saved from is sin: pride and our endless striving to be what we are not. And all of its results: fear, frustration, despair; envy, hatred, suspicion, coveting, lying, stealing, lusting, killing.

We are being saved from these by grace. We are forgiven and we forgive, and by that they are dealt with. In the final consummation when they are no more, there will be only Love: God. We shall be saved.

Indeed, you say, I should gladly believe if I were as St. Peter, St. Paul, and others who are pious and holy; but I am entirely too great a sinner. Moreover, who knows whether I am elected to salvation? Answer: Look at the words, I beseech you, to determine how and of whom He is speaking. "God so loved the world," and "that whosoever believeth in Him." Now, the "world" does not mean SS. Peter and Paul alone but the entire human race, all together. And no one is here excluded. God's Son was given for *all. All* should believe, and *all* who do believe should not perish, etc. Take hold of your own nose, I beseech you, to determine whether you are not a human being (that is, part of the world) and, like any other man, belong to the number of those comprised by the word "all." If you and I did not have to apply these words to ourselves, they must have been spoken falsely and in vain.

8

Ewald M. Plass, *What Luther Says,* Vol. II, p. 608.

In place of legalism, Jesus and Paul put the doctrine of salvation by grace through faith. The doctrine is implicit in Jesus and explicit in Paul. It is rooted in Jesus' assertion that God is a father. Every child who has loving parents knows the meaning of salvation by grace. The child does not earn his way into his parents' favor; he is loved simply because he exists. Before the child knows the meaning of love, he is surrounded with the tangible proofs of his parents' love. The true parent does not shower greater gifts upon the

8 [The doctrine of election means that God has chosen and called those who are saved. But no one should think that perhaps God has *not* chosen him, because God has called everyone to believe.]

good son than upon the less good. True family life is not built upon commercial basis of so much love for so much work; it is built freely upon grace, unearned love. The child is motivated, not by the desire to win greater favors from his parents, but by gratitude for the favors he has already received.

When the child from such a home "goes wrong," when he disappoints the hopes of his parents, he does not have to earn his way back into their favor. The parable of the Prodigal Son is [9] a beautiful presentation of salvation by grace. After the son had disgraced his home and besmirched his own and his family's good name by riotous living with harlots, he found himself hobnobbing with the pigs. As he eked out his living with husks, he decided upon a scheme to earn his way back into his father's good graces. He would become a servant in his father's home. He had a nice little speech prepared, in which he was to offer himself as a servant to his father. But his father never gave him a chance to speak it. While the son was yet far off, the father ran to him and accepted him as a son, not as a servant.

We must be careful not to interpret this too sentimentally. It is not simply a matter of letting bygones be bygones. The true parent does not simply condone the erring boy. Robert Louis Stevenson, in *The Master of Ballantrae,* has told the story of a father who did simply condone his son's sin. Stevenson says of the father that forgiveness — to misuse a noble word — flowed from him like the weak tears of senility. True parental forgiveness is not like the tears of senility; it is rather like the Cross on Golgotha; it hurts the parent; it rends his soul. It is not easy to embrace the neck that was last caressed by harlots; it is not easy to forget the scorn and the ridicule of the neighbors; but, despite the cost, the father forgives.

It is this family relationship which Jesus and Paul use to illustrate the free grace of God. God's love is not something that man has to purchase or deserve. "While we were yet sinners," says Paul, "Christ died for us" (Rom. 5:8). That is, before man had made himself good enough, God acted to save him. Through Jesus, God offers to man the promise that if he will but turn to God he will be received. This forgiveness is not an easy matter for God. Although Paul does not have any clear doctrine of the meaning of the Cross, he is certain that it represents the price that God had to pay to win man from sin. This forgiveness of God could be received by any man who would accept it in faith.

9 [See Luke 15:11-32 for the Parable of the Prodigal Son.]

Faith does not mean, for Paul, believing something, although of course some belief must be involved in it. Faith is rather a giving of oneself. The Prodigal Son had faith when he arose to go home. Faith is, for Paul, a commitment which causes one to act in a certain fashion. Faith in God did not mean believing that there was a God or believing some doctrine about Jesus; it meant giving oneself over to being a son of God, to having that mind in oneself which was in Christ Jesus (Phil. 2:5).

It would be a mistake, however, to suppose that grace was simply God's willingness to forgive the man who came to him with faith. Grace also included the power of God which comes to a man and enables him to do those things that he could not do before. Jesus asserts that faith can move mountains, and Paul concedes that through faith he has found the power that he lacked to do those things which he had known that he ought to do but which he had not done. Paul teaches that we can live "in Christ" a new life of strength and power.

The grace of God frees a man from fear and the sense of guilt. He knows that he is accepted, even as he is, by God. He knows that neither life nor death nor principalities nor powers can remove him from the love of God that is in Christ Jesus (Rom. 8:38-39). But is also frees him from the bonds of habit, indolence, and weakness that tie him to sin. Down through Christian history men have affirmed that in Christ they found two great freedoms: the freedom from fear and the freedom from sin.

William E. Hordern, *A Layman's Guide to Protestant Theology,* pp. 7, 8, 9, 1968 ed.

But we experienced the announcement as life-giving because it was an announcement, appearing in a dirty barn, and heard among the dry provincial hills and then in the forum of Rome and in the halls of royal princes and in the kitchens and streets of Paris and Calcutta and Harlem and Darien, that Joy and not Havoc is the last word. It announced to us what we could not hope. It saw limitation and contingency and disparity and irrevocability and mutability and decay and death, and it said yes, yes, yes, you are quite right: terror and horror and despair are the only eventually realistic responses . . . *if* this is all there is to it. But it is not.

You have thought of a world free from such conditions. In all your imaginings, and in your myths and your mime and your songs and dances and epics — in your quest for form and significance and beauty beyond fragmentation and inanition and chaos — you have bespoken such a vision. I announce it to you. Here, from this stable, here, from this Nazareth, this stony beach, this Jerusalem, this market place, this garden, this praetorium, this Cross, this mountain, I announce it to you.

I announce to you what is guessed at in all the phenomena of your world. You see the corn of wheat shrivel and break open and die, but you expect a crop. I tell you of the Springtime of which all springtimes speak. I tell you of the world for which this world groans and toward which it strains. I tell you that beyond the awful borders imposed by time and space and contingency, there lies what you seek. I announce to you life instead of mere existence, freedom instead of frustration, justice instead of compensation. For I announce to you redemption. Behold I make all things new. Behold I do what cannot be done. I restore the years that the locusts and worms have eaten. I restore the years which you have drooped away upon your crutches and in your wheel-chair. I restore the symphonies and operas which your deaf ears have never heard, and the snowy massif your blind eyes have never seen, and the freedom lost to you through plunder, and the identity lost to you because of calumny and the failure of justice; and I restore the good which your own foolish mistakes have cheated you of. And I bring you to the Love of which all other loves speak, the Love which is joy and beauty, and which you have sought in a thousand streets and for which you have wept and clawed your pillow.

Thomas Howard, *Christ the Tiger,* pp. 158-159.

● *Gospel*

The word "gospel" means good news. It's good news because it's grace, forgiveness, salvation. It has always been the primary word of God. He deals with man in grace. It's news because we continually creep under the Law. We feel that we must earn our worth, and we insist that other men earn our love. Then it's always news: God is love, and grace works!

So then, the gist of the Gospel is this: No man is so high or may rise so high that he need not fear becoming the lowliest. Conversely, no one has fallen, or may fall, so deeply as to preclude all hope of becoming the highest. For all merits are abolished here, and God's goodness alone is glorified. By saying: "The first shall be last" Christ takes all presumption away from you and forbids you to exalt yourself above any prostitute, even though you were Abraham, David, Peter, or Paul. But by saying: "The last shall be first" He guards you against all despair and forbids you to cast yourself under the feet of any saint, even though you were Pilate, Herod, Sodom, and Gomorrah.

Ewald M. Plass, *What Luther Says*, Vol. II, p. 613

The incredible gospel of Christianity, its tremendous Good News, is that God Himself in human form has come into the human scene, has stood and still stands not against but beside man in his human plight, has suffered and died not only for man but with man, to the end that any who will may be liberated into a new life which is nothing less than a rising from the dead. This Good News is summed up in the death and resurrection of Jesus Christ, a scandal to reason, but the power of God to them that believe *in Him.*

Lewis Joseph Sherrill, *Guilt and Redemption*, p. 164.

What is the Gospel but the sermon that Christ gave Himself for us that He might save us from sin, that all who believe this might certainly be saved in this manner, and that thus sinners, despairing of their own efforts, might cling to Christ alone and rely on Him? This is a very lovely and consoling declaration and readily enters such hearts as are despondent about their own efforts. Therefore the word "evangel" means a sweet, kind, and gracious message which gladdens and cheers a sorrowful and terrified heart.

Ewald M. Plass, *What Luther Says,* Vol. II, p. 562

With this fear of the Lord before our eyes we address our appeal to men. To God our lives lie open, as I hope they also lie open to you in your heart of hearts. This is not another attempt to recommend ourselves to you: we are rather giving you a chance to show yourselves proud of us; then you will have something to say to those whose pride is all in outward show and not in inward worth. It may be we are beside ourselves, but it is for God; if we are in our right mind, it is for you. For the love of Christ leaves us no choice, when once we have reached the conclusion that one man died for all and therefore all mankind has died. His purpose in dying for all was that men, while still in life, should cease to live for themselves, and should live for Him who for their sake died and was raised to life. With us therefore worldly standards have ceased to count in our estimate of any man; even if once they counted in our understanding of Christ, they do so now no longer. When anyone is united to Christ, there is a new world; the old order has gone, and a new order has already begun.

From first to last this has been the work of God. He has reconciled us men to himself through Christ, and he has enlisted us in this service of reconciliation. What I mean is, that God was in Christ reconciling the world to himself, no longer holding men's misdeeds against them, and that he has entrusted us with the message of reconciliation. We come therefore as Christ's ambassadors. It is as if God were appealing to you through us: in Christ's name, we implore you, be reconciled to God! Christ was innocent of sin, and yet for our sake God made him one with the sinfulness of men, so that in him we might be made one with the goodness of God himself. Sharing in God's work, we urge this appeal upon you: you have received the grace of God; do not let it go for nothing. God's own words are:

> "In the hour of my favour I gave heed to you;
> On the day of deliverance I came to your aid."

The hour of favour has now come; now, I say, has the day of deliverance dawned.

2 Corinthians 5:11 — 6:2 NEB

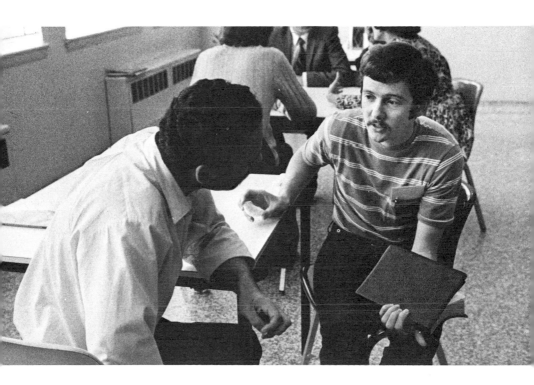

COMMUNITY: THE PEOPLE OF GOD

Community is a human need, not just a church arrangement. God works with us in our need: He calls a family, a nation, a people, a church to be His ambassador. We can join something!

God's community works among men according to the rules and patterns of any human community—but with God's strength and God's direction. We have human organization, human rituals, human weakness. But in it all God works. His purpose is that He might be known among men, and that men might be reconciled to Him in grace.

Let us be concerned with one another, to help one another to show love and to do good. Let us not give up the habit of meeting together, as some are doing. Instead, let us encourage one another, all the more since you see that the Day of the Lord is coming near.

Hebrews 10:24, 25, TEV

God has willed that we should seek and find His living Word in the witness of a brother, in the mouth of man. Therefore, the Christian needs another Christian who speaks God's Word to him. He needs him again and again when he becomes uncertain and discouraged, for by himself he cannot help himself without belying the truth. He needs his brother man as a bearer and proclaimer of the divine word of salvation. He needs his brother solely because of Jesus Christ. The Christ in his own heart is weaker than the Christ in the word of his brother; his own heart is uncertain, his brother's is sure.

Dietrich Bonhoeffer, *Life Together,* p. 23

It is our human weakness that must be acknowledged, our immense need for support. If we search for success, or truth, it is not only for the pleasure of success and the contemplation of truth, but also in order to reassure ourselves in our weakness and to lean on the success and on the truths we have discovered. We feel weak, and would all like to be stronger than we are. That is why we imagine other people to be stronger than they really are. It is because we are all weak that both they and we cling to our support, and dare not let go in order to press forward; and it is in this inability to let go that we experience our weakness. . . .

All men are looking, in fact, for God's support. Some are quite aware of the fact; in others it is only a vague nostalgic longing. Some seek it openly, seriously, and humbly; others hide what they are doing behind a façade of pleasantries or oaths. It is the only support that measures up to their infinite need for security.

Paul Tournier, *A Place for You,* pp. 184, 197

Many people seek fellowship because they are afraid to be alone. Because they cannot stand loneliness, they are driven to seek the company of other people. There are Christians, too, who cannot endure being alone, who have had some bad experiences with themselves, who hope they will gain some help in association with others. They are generally disappointed. Then they blame the fellowship for what is really their own fault. The Christian community is not a spiritual sanatorium. The person who comes into a fellowship because he is running away from himself is misusing it for the sake of diversion, no matter how spiritual this diversion may appear. He is really not seeking community at all, but only distraction which will allow him to forget his loneliness for a brief time, the very alienation that creates the deadly isolation of man. The disintegration of communication and all genuine experience, and finally resignation and spiritual death are the result of such attempts to find a cure.

Let him who cannot be alone beware of community. He will only do harm to himself and to the community. Alone you stood before God when he called you; alone you had to answer that call; alone you had to struggle and pray; and alone you will die and give an account to God. You cannot escape from yourself; for God has singled you out. If you refuse to be alone you are rejecting Christ's call to you, and you can have no part in the community of those who are called. "The challenge of death comes to us all, and no one can die for another. Everyone must fight his own battle with death by himself, alone. . . . I will not be with you then, nor you with me" (Luther).

But the reverse is also true: *Let him who is not in community beware of being alone.* Into the community you were called, the call was not meant for you alone; in the community of the called you bear your cross, you struggle, you pray. You are not alone, even in death, and on the Last Day you will be only one member of the great congregation of Jesus Christ. If you scorn the fellowship of the brethren, you reject the call of Jesus Christ, and thus your solitude can only be hurtful to you. "If I die, then I am not alone in death; if I suffer they [the fellowship] suffer with me" (Luther).

We recognize, then, that only as we are within the fellowship can we be alone, and only he that is alone can live in the fellowship. Only in the fellowship do we learn to be rightly alone and only in aloneness do we learn to live rightly in the fellowship. It is not as though the one preceded the other; both begin at the same time, namely, with the call of Jesus Christ.

Each by itself has profound pitfalls and perils. One who wants fellowship without solitude plunges into the void of words and feelings, and one who seeks solitude without fellowship perishes in the abyss of vanity, self-infatuation, and despair.

Dietrich Bonhoeffer, *Life Together,* pp. 76-78

● CHURCH PEOPLE

*The church is a community of people. But not all people
communities are church. It may not always be easy to tell the
difference, but there are marks by which you can say, "These with
whom I pray are moved by the Spirit of my God."*

What's wrong with the people in church?
What's the matter with them, Lord?
What happens to people
when they get inside a church?
Why do they change
and freeze up
when they get inside a church?
They don't seem to enjoy themselves
or talk to anyone.

They freeze up tight.
I know
because I've been watching them.
They look like penguins
standing on the shore
and staring at the weary ocean.

I watch them mumble through a melody
they've sung a thousand times or more
the way their tired parents sang it
for fifty years before.

I watch them turn to pray
by closing in their eyes
or staring at the floor
or gazing at the covered legs
of the person in the pew ahead.
I see them waiting for a miracle
when the preacher says his piece,
his one precious capsule
that's supposed to save their lives
for one more week.

I watch them watching one another
as they waddle down the aisle,

returning from a sip
of supermarket wine.

I watch them watching one another
and I wonder what they're thinking
about each other's clothes
and self-conscious faces,
or about that guy
who folds his hands
as if they're glued
underneath his chin.

To be honest with you, God,
I'm so thankful
I'm not like other people in church,
like the Peters or the Schmidts,
especially the Schmidts.

I know quite well
that I come to church
and act the part as others do.
But that's different . . .
isn't it?

Or are the other people in church
really like me anyway?
Are they?
Are they rebellious kids at heart,
afraid to change
the way they act in church
because it's easier that way?

Will the people in church
ever change?

Will they?

Norman C. Habel, *For Mature Adults Only,* pp. 54, 55

We should with certainty recognize the presence of the
Christian Church wherever the pure Gospel is being preached. For
just as we recognize by the flag, as a certain sign, which lord and
army are keeping the field, so we by the Gospel also recognize with
certainty where Christ and His army are. We have a sure promise
from God to this effect in Is. 55:10-11. . . .

Therefore we are certain that it is impossible that there are no Christians where the Gospel is preached, however few and frail and sinful they may be. Just so it is impossible that there are any Christians where the Gospel is not preached but where human doctrine is in control. There only pagans can be, however numerous the people may be and however holy and fine their conduct may be.

Ewald M. Plass, *What Luther Says,* Vol. I, pp. 263, 264

The Christian church and the Holy Spirit are closely allied, for it is the Spirit who came in fullest measure on the Day of Pentecost. As he somehow in a mysterious manner guided people to gather the documents of the Bible, so he led men and women and children into a community of love, a fellowship of the Spirit, a communion of saints, which more and more came to be known as the church. Need we pause to underscore here that the church is not a building or even primarily an organization but a group of people who confess that Christ is their Lord? . . .

Where Christ is, there is the church. Many definitions have been given of the church, but this seems to be valid: Christ and his church ought not to be separated. The church has a divine purpose, and the degree to which she serves God she is the church. The Holy Spirit is eager and ready to build a community of love among us as vital and authentic and relevant as any in the past. Every reformation rests on the work of the Holy Spirit, and it may well be [1] that the next great reformation will come when we shall be ready to receive in fuller measure what the Spirit has to offer.

But the church is for imperfect people, and hence she can and does make miserable mistakes. This was true already in the first century, when the apostles had to remind Christians not to give special honor to the wealthy in the Sunday service and that incest is not to be condoned in the fellowship of Christ. You will recall other instances of this kind.

William D. Streng, *In Search of Ultimates,* pp. 58, 59

The church is the means which God chooses for saving the world. This is its purpose. The church is the result of the mighty acts of God in the life and death and resurrection of Jesus Christ, by

---

[1] [Periodically, the church needs reforming because it is made up of imperfect men. Such reformations are accomplished by God through the men He gives us as leaders.]

which something decisive for the whole of history took place.
Presumably, God could have chosen other means; we simply confess
that it is through the church that the event is to be proclaimed
to men, both by the life and work of the church. Jesus did not leave
behind primarily a code of ethics or a set of principles for life,
but a group of men who were bound together by their knowledge
that he was their Lord and Savior. "As thou didst send me into
the world, so I have sent them into the world." (John 17:18.)

The Christian community, a body of those called from darkness into light by the power of God's grace, exists to *worship* and to *witness*. The whole life of the church must revolve around these foci. To give glory to God by its corporate worship and sacramental life and to serve his purpose by its existence as a colony in the world— these define the whole meaning of the church's life.

George W. Webber, *God's Colony in Man's World,* pp. 43, 51, 52

The church is recognized, not by external peace but by the Word and the Sacraments. For wherever you see a small group that has the true Word and the Sacraments, there the church is if only the pulpit and the baptismal font are pure. The church does not stand on the holiness of any one person but solely on the holiness and righteousness of the Lord Christ, for He has sanctified her by Word and Sacrament.

2

Ewald M. Plass, *What Luther Says,* Vol. I, p. 263

The inner man is a saint; the outer man is a sinner. That is why we confess in the Creed that the church is holy but pray for forgiveness of sins in the Lord's Prayer.

3

Ewald M. Plass, *What Luther Says,* Vol. I, p. 236

Luke testifies (Acts 15:39) that a dissension so sharp arose between Paul and Barnabas . . . that the one left the other. Here either Paul or Barnabas went too far. It must have been a violent disagreement to separate these associates who were so closely united. Indeed, the text indicates as much. Such examples are written for our consolation; for it is a great comfort to us to hear that great saints, who have the Spirit of God, also sin. Of this comfort those would deprive us who say that saints do not sin. Samson, David, and many other celebrated men full of the Holy

[2] [In the Bible, "righteousness" means being in a right relationship with God. Among Christians, the word means having and living in the forgiving grace of Jesus Christ. "Sanctified" means "made holy or righteous." We are sanctified by the Word and Sacrament because in them we know and receive God's grace. The word "sacrament" is explained in the next section of this book.]

[3] [By the "inner man" Luther means the believing heart in which we accept the idea of grace. By the "outer man" he means the daily life in which we fail to live up to our faith.]

Spirit fell into grievous sins. Job and Jeremiah cursed the day of
their birth (Job 3:3 ff.; Jer. 20:14); Elijah and Jonah are weary of life
and desire death (1 Kings 19:4; Jonah 4:8). . . . No man has ever
fallen so grievously but that he might have risen again. Conversely,
no man stands so firmly but that he may fall. If Peter fell, I, too,
may fall; if he rose again, I, too, may rise again (Matt. 26:70).

Ewald M. Plass, *What Luther Says,* Vol. III, p. 1,249

● *Baptism*

*God has given us two sacred acts to identify and strengthen us.
They are an integral part of our worship together. In Baptism God
names you as a member of the body He has called to make Him
known. In the Eucharist He assures you of His presence and
forgiveness in your mission. In worship you celebrate the mystery
of your salvation and your calling.*

Baptism I think is the foundational sacrament and the
foundational act in the church, not because singly and by itself
it should have so much attention paid to it, but because it is
a microcosm of all that the gospel is. It is a mirror of grace. It
embodies in it all the aspects that one would want mentioned when
one explains the gospel. . . .
It is a microcosm of the gospel because God acts on my behalf
before and without my knowledge. God has done something for me
quite outside my need for it or my desire for it or my understanding
of it. God justifies the ungodly. God's grace is for the unlovely.
(You can say it in a thousand ways.) Whenever you have an adult
involved with the mind, the decision, commitment, and understanding
and all that's involved is difficult to pinpoint, but in infant baptism
it is clear. God asks for this child without the child's understanding,
without its knowledge, without its wishes, without any decisions,
therefore the gospel is illustrated. *Pure* grace is demonstrated more
than any other place. I think infant baptism has a tremendous value;
I think it is a constant reminder to the church that this is what
grace is. If we didn't have infant baptism then we would have lost
one of the great symbols of the gospel.

From a paper, "Baptism and Christian Education," by Kent Knutson

The relationships established by baptism may best be understood in the relationship established by adoption. If my wife and I adopt a child there are some commitments to be made—of public record.

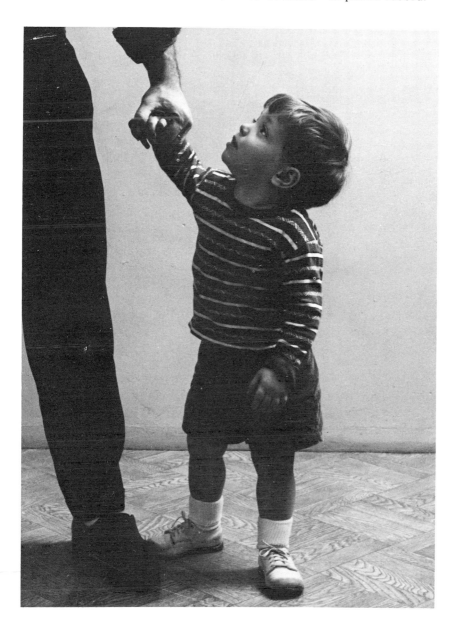

And then the great act takes place. The child is declared to be our child—an Evenson. He is responsible to us and we are responsible for him. He is heir to all that we have. He is part of our family. But since he is an infant, he does not know it. Someone will have to tell him. All who surround him—who will help him to learn to walk and then to talk and then to read and then to get along with people and then to find what he can best do in his life—all who help him—brothers and sisters, teachers and leaders, relatives, neighbors, and friends—all who are near to him have a great job to do—to help him catch on to who he *is*—and what that identity means for his life.

And that task cannot be accomplished by some prayers over his crib, nor by an announcement to him some day, nor by word of correction, an act of example, an answer to a question, a comment on an event, or even a series of lessons. But little by little, through all of these, over and over again in each successive stage of life, the adopted one becomes more and more, in his own feelings and experiences, what he was declared to be on the day of the adoption.

C. Richard Evenson, unpublished Ms.

It is treacherous to underscore any one aspect of the Sacraments at the expense of all others. Certainly, they are gifts of a loving Father.

This needs to be said, for infant baptism is under severe attack today. Yet if Baptism is a gift, dare we ask: "Must children be baptized?" We might as well ask, "Must I accept my Christmas gifts?" One never uses the word "must" when a gift is at stake. If Baptism is a gift of God's love would he not be eager to share this with everyone? Does God love infants?

Yet there is a valid reason for such concerted criticism of infant baptism, since it has so easily become a matter of "cheap grace." Recently a group of young pastors deliberately refused to have their own infants baptized in order to bear testimony to the fact that in church circles Baptism has often become a mere "form." Baptism of one's child may mean suffering and persecution for him, self-sacrifice and ostracism; hence we may wish to walk a bit more slowly to the baptismal font (cf. 2 Timothy 3:12).

For Baptism is a covenant. The nature of this covenant can be compared to a marriage, as in the Book of Hosea or as an adoption by God (1 Peter 2:9). One can become a deserter or a prostitute in this matter.

How God took the initiative and how superior this covenant of Baptism is to the one established in the Old Testament is portrayed graphically in the Epistle to the Hebrews. . . .

Another reason why Baptism has lost some of its intrinsic power is that the close relationship between "teach and baptize" has too easily been overlooked. Without instruction Baptism becomes a meaningless rite with superstitious connotations. This emphasis is so strong that a renowned theologian has concluded that we ought never baptize an infant when there is no promise of further instruction, as for instance when it is certain that an infant will not live. Whole portions of the New Testament were written as manuals of instruction for Baptism. Study of these documents is neither a fad nor an option for those who take their Baptism seriously, for there is nothing obscure in Christ's command to "teach and baptize."

The gifts of Baptism may be variously interpreted — forgiveness, adoption, the Holy Spirit, new life — and can always be discussed with profit, provided they lead to mission. In some churches the rite   4
of confirmation is closely associated with Baptism. This has value if meaningful instruction becomes the major thrust and confirmation itself a call to service, like a soldier's induction into an army that is equipped to go out to serve. Present practices in this area are under severe scrutiny.

William D. Streng, *In Search of Ultimates,* pp. 84 – 86

The sacrament of Baptism as a means of grace is a miracle of God performed through the church. By this act God lays claim on the sinner.

God's relationship with the sinner is so radically changed by Baptism that the Bible calls the experience a new birth (John 3:5). Man is said to become a new person (Titus 3:5; 2 Corinthians 5:17). The old person who is under the judgment of God dies and a new person who is under forgiveness and grace is born (Romans 6:4; Acts 2:38, 22:16).

Baptism also gives the sinner a new relationship with the church. It makes him fully a member of the church (1 Corinthians 12:13). It gives him the gift of the Holy Spirit (Titus 3:5).

The saving benefit of Baptism is entirely God's doing. It is

---

4 ["Mission" here means the realization that we are *sent* by God to do His work on earth. "Confirmation" is the ceremony in which a person publicly enters the adult fellowship of the church.]

prompted solely by his love and mercy. It is not conditioned in any
way by any decision or promise or act of man, whether by his
parents or sponsors, or by himself as in a confirmation rite. To
assert or even to imply that the saving power of Baptism is in any
way contingent on any subsequent event is to deny its status. It is
therefore theologically indefensible to give a confirmation rite
a meaning whereby it is elevated to a position in which it either
complements or supplements the sacrament of Holy Baptism.

By his own free grace God brings man into a child-father
relationship or he can ignore it. In either event, as Luther said,
"Baptism remains forever. Even though we fall from it and sin,
nevertheless we always have access to it" (*The Large Catechism,*
IV, 77). What man does is in response to an act that is complete in
itself. The responsibility of the Christian, therefore, with respect to
the relationship given him in Baptism, is to learn to know it, live in
response to it, enjoy it, and celebrate it. For this reason, Baptism
itself implies the need for a lifelong process of education through
which the believer grows within his baptismal relationship.

---

*The Report of the Joint Commission on the Theology and Practice of
Confirmation,* p. 14; cf. *Confirmation and First Communion: a Study
Book,* p. 193.

 # WORSHIP

In the worship service the congregation comes together, on the
command and promise of God, to be assured of the Lord's presence
in Word and Sacrament. When the Word of God is proclaimed
clearly and purely and the Sacraments are administered according
to the command of Christ, we experience the fullness of the grace
of the present Lord. There the Spirit calls, gathers, enlightens,
sanctifies, and preserves Christendom. There the congregation
comes before the Triune God in confident petition, intercession, and
thankfulness, and in adoration of his glory. It praises God in its
singing and brings to him its offering.

In worship the congregation transcends all divisions and is
united with Christians of all times and places and with the hosts
before the throne of God. In the midst of the world it awaits the
coming of the Lord.

J. Bodensieck, *Encyclopedia of the Lutheran Church,* p. 2,524

And we experienced his announcement as death dealing again, because it knocked over all the little pickets and wickets that we had tapped carefully into place to guarantee the safety of our religion. He saw our masses and rosaries and prayer meetings and study groups and devotions, and he said yes, yes, yes, you are quite right to think that goodness demands rigor and vigilance and observance, but your new moons and sabbaths and bullocks and altars and vestments and Gospel teams and taboos and Bible studies are trumpery, and they nauseate me because you have elevated *them,* and I alone am the Host. Your incense is foetid, and your annotated Bibles are rubbish paper. Your meetings are a bore and your myopic exegesis is suffocating. Return, return, and think again what I have asked of you: to follow justice, and love mercy, and do your job of work, and love one another, and give me the worship of your heart — your *heart* — and be merry and thankful and lowly and not pompous and gaunt and sere.

Thomas Howard, *Christ the Tiger,* pp. 157 – 158

Endless experiments are being conducted to discover the relevance of meaningful worship. Recall that one of the first acts of Martin Luther was to make available to his contemporaries a worship service which they could understand and in which they could participate. To what degree liturgy or fixed formal services help or hinder has not been determined and may vary with situations and people. But it is one of the hopeful signs that jazz and Bach and chanting and guitars are used today to glorify God in worship.

William D. Streng, *In Search of Ultimates,* pp. 83, 84

V

I say to my son, these are the visible and outward forms,
These are the inarticulate gestures, the humble and supplicating
    hands of the blind reached out,

---

[5] [Several words in this paragraph may be obscure. "Pickets and wickets" is a play on words referring to the sticks driven into the ground in the game of cricket, which the bowler tries to knock apart. In the sentence beginning "He saw our masses and rosaries . . ." all of the terms refer to the ceremonies that we have made for our worship. We tend to worship (elevate) them rather than God. "Myopic exegesis" means "near-sighted interpretation of the Bible."]

This is the reaching out of children's hands for the wild bird, these
    are the hands stretched out for water in the dry and barren land.
This is the searching in a forest for a treasure, buried long since
    under a tree with branches,
This is the searching in the snowstorm for the long-waited letter, the
    lost white paper that has blown away,
This is the savage seeking a tune from the harp, the man raking the
    ashes for the charm in the burned-down house.
This is man thrusting his head through the stars, searching the void
    for the Incomprehensible and Holy;
Keep for it always your reverence and earnestness, these are men
    searching here,
They stretch out their hands for no star, for no knowledge however
    weighty,
They reach out humbly, supplicating, not more than a cubit's length
That haply they may touch the hem of the robe of the infinite and   6
    Everlasting God.

VI

This kneeling, this singing, this reading from ancient books,   7
This acknowledgment that the burden is intolerable, this promise
    of amendment,
This humble access, this putting out of the hands,
This taking of the bread and wine, this return to your place not
    glancing about you,
This solemn acceptance and the thousand sins that will follow it,
    this thousand sins and the repenting of them,
This dedication and this apostasy, this apostasy and this restoration,
This thousand restorations and this thousand apostasies,
Take and accept them all, be not affronted nor dismayed by them.
They are a net of holes to capture essence, a shell to house the
    thunder of an ocean,
A discipline of petty acts to catch Creation, a rune of words to hold
    One Living Word,

6 [See Luke 8:43-44.]

7 [The terms in the first seven lines of this section are taken from the rite of the
Eucharist in the church of the author. "Humble access" means coming to the altar
for the Communion. "Apostasy" means the loss of faith. In the second to last line,
"rune" means an ancient ceremonial repetition of words.]

A Ladder built by men of sticks and stones, whereby they hope to reach to heaven.

"Meditation for a Young Boy Confirmed," by Alan Paton, in *The Christian Century*, October 13, 1954, p. 1,237

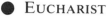 EUCHARIST

The day of the Lord's Supper is an occasion of joy for the Christian community. Reconciled in their hearts with God and the brethren, the congregation receives the gift of the body and blood of Jesus Christ, and, receiving that, it receives forgiveness, new life, and salvation. It is given new fellowship with God and men. The fellowship of the Lord's Supper is the superlative fulfillment of Christian fellowship. As the members of the congregation are united in body and blood at the table of the Lord so will they be together in eternity. Here the community has reached its goal. Here joy in Christ and his community is complete. The life of Christians together under the Word has reached its perfection in the sacrament.

Dietrich Bonhoeffer, *Life Together*, p. 122

XI

Such was the brief, such was the lonely life,
Such was the bondage of the earth, such was the misery,
Such was the reaching out, such was the separation,
That my Lord tore the curtain from the skies, and in compassion
He took upon Himself all angry things, the scourge, the thorn, the
    nail, the utter separation;
And spoke such words as made me tremble, and laid His yoke
    upon me
And bound me with these chains, that I have worn with no
    especial grace.
Why then I did accept this miracle, and being what I am some
    lesser miracles,
And then I did accept this Faith, and being what I am some certain
    Articles,
And then I did accept this Law, and being what I am some
    regulations,
Why then I worshiped Him, and being what I am knelt in some pew

And heard some organ play and some bells peal, and heard some
    people sing,
And heard about some money that was wanted, and heard some sin
    was preached against,
And heard some message given by some man, sometimes with great
    distinction, sometimes none.
I made this humble access, I too stretched out my hands,
Sometimes I saw Him not, and sometimes clearly, though with my
    inward eyes.
I stayed there on my knees, I saw His feet approaching,
I saw the mark of the nails, I did not dare to look fully at them
I longed to behold Him, I did not dare to behold Him,
I said in my heart to Him, I who in sins and doubts and in my
    grievous separation reach out my hands,
Reach out Thy hands and touch me, oh most Holy One.

"Meditation for a Young Boy Confirmed," by Alan Paton, in *The Christian
Century,* October 13, 1954, p. 1,239

● SERVICE

The Christian, however, must bear the burden of a brother. He
must suffer and endure the brother. It is only when he is a burden
that another person is really a brother and not merely an object to be
manipulated. The burden of men was so heavy for God Himself that
He had to endure the Cross. God verily bore the burden of men in
the body of Jesus Christ. But He bore them as a mother carries her
child, as a shepherd enfolds the lost lamb that has been found. God
took men upon Himself and they weighted Him to the ground, but
God remained with them and they with God. In bearing with men
God maintained fellowship with them. It is the law of Christ that
was fulfilled in the Cross. And Christians must share in this law.
They must suffer their brethren, but, what is more important, now
that the law of Christ has been fulfilled, they *can* bear with their
brethren.

Dietrich Bonhoeffer, *Life Together,* p. 100

I pray, "Come into my heart, Lord Jesus" — and he comes. But he does not come alone. He brings with him people who are in need — the hungry, the sick, the unwanted. And he asks, "Did you want to do something for me? Then do for these, my brothers."

I had counted on his coming alone. We could have had a cozy and warm hour, just we two. I would have liked to hear his voice alone — not the groans and cries of these unloved and unloving of the world.

Any time we come within earshot of Jesus' voice, we risk hearing the wailing voices of the world's unfortunate.

We had better not enter the door of the church if we want to be left alone. At this very moment, as you read these lines, there is a knocking at your door. Christ knocks and with him the needy world. Your church, with its programs and budgets, offers you a way. The gifts you give in the offering plate is indeed one way. For these gifts will flow through a bank deposit out into the work of love to the uttermost parts of the earth.

Writing a check is but one way. You are not done when the offering plate has gone by. God recruits more than money. He recruits your prayers, your time, your skills, your heart. He points you to the man next door, the discouraged families in your neighborhood, the sick and forgotten in hospitals, your son's friend from a failing home. All these the Lord brings with him as he enters your heart.

It's a terrifying thing to let him in. But what is your life for, if not to bear the burdens of others? And as you lift their load, they may catch a glimpse of the Christ. They will thank you, and they may lift their eyes to glorify the God who sent you.

Alvin Rogness, *Captured by Mystery*, pp. 34, 35

The ministry of the church as the Body of Christ in the world is the same as the ministry of Christ. The ministry of Christ is the ministry of a servant in the world and for the world — a servant of the world in the name of God.

Perhaps it is helpful to notice a few things about the ministry of Christ. One is that the ministry of Christ is a ministry of great extravagance — of a reckless, scandalous expenditure of His life for the sake of the world's life. Christ gives away His life. The world finds new life in His life and in His gift of His life to the world. His is not a very prudential life, not a very conservative life, not a very cautious life, not — by ordinary standards — a very successful life.

He shunned no one, not even adulterers, not even tax collectors, not even neurotics and psychotics, not even those tempted to suicide, not even alcoholics, not even poor people, not even beggars, not even lepers, not even those who ridiculed Him, not even those who betrayed Him, not even His own enemies. He shunned no one.

The words that tell of the ministry of Christ are words of sorrow, poverty, rejection, radical unpopularity. They are words of agony.

It seems ridiculous to apply such words to the ministry of churches nowadays. Yet where these words cannot be truthfully applied to the ministry of the churches today they must then be spoken against the churches to show how far the churches are from being the Body of Christ engaged in the ministry of Christ in the world.

The Church exists as the company of participants in God's witness to Himself in the world. The Church exists for the sake of the world into which God enters and in which He acts and for which He expends His own life.

William Stringfellow, *A Private and Public Faith,* pp. 83, 84

This provides the highly popular slogan of the "servant church" with a new dimension. Although the church will remain a human institution, it is not to seek its own glory. It will resist the temptations to arrogance and self-sufficiency in any of their forms: the crass temptations to glory in size, possessions, or power; the more subtle temptations to make churchly means ends in themselves; the temptations to be the final instructor of the world because of its wisdom or goodness. Thus the church recognizes the fact that it is composed of sinful people whose faith is often small and whose vision is often narrow. But unlike the world, the church should be living out a process of placing its life under the judgment and grace of God. The church should be enacting the dynamics of repentance and thus of continuing transformation. May we emphasize again that the church is not pointing to itself as the source of renewal but to the One who gives power and freedom? Throughout its history the church has never fully succeeded in living an authentic life. As a human institution it has frequently conformed to its surrounding environment. Yet the church has endured; the Gospel has been proclaimed and lives have been transformed; love has been demonstrated; and at its highest points the church has been ready to lay down its life in behalf of those in need.

David S. Schuller, *Power Structures and the Church*, p. 55

I believe that I cannot
    by my own understanding or effort
believe in Jesus Christ, my Lord,
    or come to Him.
But the Holy Spirit has called me
    through the Gospel,
enlightened me with His gifts,
and sanctified and kept me in true faith.

In the same way He calls, gathers,
    enlightens, and sanctifies
the whole Christian church on earth,
and keeps it united with Jesus Christ
    in the one true faith.

In this Christian church day after day
He fully forgives my sins
and the sins of all believers.
On the last day He will raise me and all
        the dead
and give me and all believers in Christ
        eternal life.
This is most certainly true.

Martin Luther, The Small Catechism

The word "church" is a translation of the Greek word "ekklesia" which refers to a body of people, not so much assembling because they have chosen to come together, but assembling because God has called them to Himself: not so much to share their own thoughts and opinions, but assembling to listen to the voice of God.

But the New Testament uses a number of other pictures and images to visualize and describe the church. Some of these include:

Saints	Ephesians 1:1
Disciples	Acts 14:21, 22
Children of God	1 John 3:1-3
Brotherhood	1 Peter 2:17
Household	Ephesians 2:19
	Galatians 6:10
People of God	1 Peter 2:9, 10
Slaves/Servants	Romans 6:22
	Galatians 5:13
Flock	1 Peter 5:2
Body of Christ	Romans 12:4, 5
	Ephesians 5:23
Bride	Ephesians 5:25-32
Chosen People	1 Peter 2:9
	1 Corinthians 1:26-29

Come with me.
It is the childish custom
of the little of heart
to gather strength
and to multiply the volume of their courage
by going with someone
little of heart.
Come, coward, be brave enough
to enlist the bravery of another coward.
Together you may be heroes.
In the beginning of cowardice
God understood,
It is not good for man to be alone.
He created the law of bravery
for lonely
cowards and honest men.
This law has been obeyed in every generation
as the children of men
find themselves in new corridors.
It is a law broken and obeyed
in Gethsemane,
in the huge bid for companionship.
Courage, cowards of Gethsemane.
Come with Me
for just this hour.

Herbert F. Brokering and Joseph Zimbolt, *Lifetimes*, p. 47

8 [In His last hours in the Garden of Gethsemane, Jesus asked His disciples to
"watch with Him," part of the celebration of fellowship in the Hebrew Passover
festival.]

THE WORD: THE REVELATION OF GOD

When we say "the Word of God" one of the first mental images formed is the Bible. But even the Bible points out that God has been expressing Himself from the very beginning in very many ways. Even the act of creating expresses the grace of God, the same grace expressed in Jesus Christ. Creation is a word of God. Jesus is the Word of God. Every way in which we come nearer to understanding grace is a word of God.

The Bible is unique as a word. Creation is a unique word. Jesus is the only Son, a unique Word. One mother's love for her child is unique. It would be silly to say that all these "words" are the same. It would be just as foolish to say that God has spoken only once, in only one way.

In the past God spoke to our ancestors many times and in many ways through the prophets, but in these last days he has spoken to us through his Son. God made him the owner of all things, and through him God created the universe.

Hebrews 1:1, 2, TEV, 1966

People think: If I could hear God speaking in His own Person, I would run so fast to hear Him that my feet would bleed. . . . If in former times someone had said: I know of a place in the world where God speaks, and when you arrive there, you hear God Himself talking; and if I had come there, had seen a poor preacher baptize and preach, and people had said: This is the place; there God is speaking through the preacher: he is teaching God's Word — then I no doubt would have said: Ha! I have taken pains to come here, and I see only a minister! We should like to have God speak with us in His majesty; but I advise you: Do not go there. So experience certainly teaches. If He were to speak in His majesty, you would see what a running would begin, as there at Mount Sinai, where, after all, only the angels spoke; yet the mountain smoked and trembled. But now you have the Word of God in church, in books, in your home; and this is as certainly God's Word as if God Himself were speaking.

Ewald M. Plass, *What Luther Says,* Vol. III, p. 1,461

Where do you hear God? You either hear him everywhere, or you hear him nowhere. To hear him everywhere, however, you must first hear him in Jesus Christ. He is a local voice before he becomes a universal voice. You hear him in one place before you hear him in every place. This is how God has elected to reveal himself to men.

God remains a vague, mysterious, and hidden power—and therefore not God at all—until you have him in the person of someone who has walked the ways of men.

The roar of the waterfall remains but a roar, the whisper of the winds in the trees is but a whisper. Nature speaks but her own language, unless you have heard God speak to you through the Savior-Lord.

Happy is the man who has had his ears opened by the living Word in Christ. Then everything begins to speak of God. Knowing his love, you can know his majesty. Knowing his love, you can see his handiwork in the intricate and complex design of all creation.

Even the revelation of God in Christ is but a clue to the wonder and mystery of God. It is a sufficient clue—adequate for our salvation—but, at best, we can but touch the hem of the garment of the majesty and glory of God.

How dull and prosaic life would be if there were no mystery! How dark and terrifying if there were no clue at all to the mystery! God remains the hidden God at the very moment he discloses himself in Jesus of Nazareth. We see him and yet we do not see him. We walk by faith, therefore, and what a walk that is!

It is in the Bible that we find him and hear him. But it is in the Bible that we confront the wonder of a love and peace which remain forever beyond our understanding. Out from the Bible we turn to find and hear him everywhere.

Alvin Rogness, *Captured by Mystery,* pp. 126, 127

Word of God is probably the phrase Christians most commonly use to indicate that the Bible is a divinely inspired revelation. Like revelation and inspiration, Word of God locates the source of what is communicated in God, but also emphasizes events in history and human personalities.

When we think of words, we usually mean verbs, nouns, and the other parts of speech we combine into sentences to express ideas. When the Bible says "God spoke," does this mean people heard God speak words as they hear people speak words? Or was God's way of communicating so difficult to describe that biblical writers had to resort to a figure of speech? The Bible itself does not answer our question. As usual, it is more concerned with source and result than with process.

We are not without clues, however. In Isaiah 2:1 we read of the word which Isaiah "saw." Isaiah either saw a vision or witnessed an event. The latter is quite possible, since the Hebrew for "word" also means "happening" or "act." (Note again how appropriate is our course title, "The Mighty Acts of God.")

A second clue to the meaning of Word of God appears in the opening chapter of John's Gospel where Christ is called the "Word." Here to know the Word is to know God as a living person. Knowing a person is more than having certain ideas about him. It also involves feelings; you are attracted or repelled, you love or you hate. Thus as the Word of God the Bible confronts us with the living God and calls for the response such a confrontation requires.

Paul made this clear when he wrote, ". . . our gospel came to you not only in word, but also in power and in the Holy Spirit" (1 Thessalonians 1:5). To know God is not to have an idea, but to live in a relationship with a personal being. We shall need to keep this in mind as we think of the Bible as the Word of God.

Robert J. Marshall, *The Mighty Acts of God*, pp. 15, 16

The story of the making of the Bible is a story which enables us to see the supreme value of the books of the Bible as nothing else can or does. It enables us to see that these books did not become Scripture by the decision of any Church or any man; they became Scripture because out of them men in their sorrow found comfort, in their despair hope, in their weakness strength, in their temptations power, in their darkness light, in their uncertainty faith, and in their sin a Saviour. That is why the Bible is the word of God. When the Church did make its canonical lists, it was not choosing and selecting these books; it was only affirming and attesting that these already were the books on which men had stayed their hearts and fed their

souls. And that is why there never can be a time when the Church
or the Christian can do without this Bible which had always been the
word of God to His people, and the place where men find Jesus
Christ.

William Barclay, *The Making of the Bible*, pp. 93, 94

If John were here, he would say to us: "Don't get so hysterical
about the difficulties of your era. Take a longer view. See what God
has been doing from the beginning and what a long, bitter,
discouraging struggle it has been to get as far as we have come.
God has a design. The world is not at the mercy of a blind,
relentless fate; the world is still God's creation, created and shaped
by him through his Word, able to rebel against his purpose and
design for it, but not able to deliver itself out of his hand."
But how can we know what this design is that God has for the
world? How can we believe in it unless we see it? God has already
shown it to us. His Word, his design, was made flesh in Jesus Christ.
The clue to the meaning of all history is in this one little segment of
history that is enclosed by the birth and life and death and
resurrection of Jesus. It is here at this one point that you find the
meaning both of your own personal history and of the world's
history. It is here that you can discover what God is doing with our
troubled and distressed humanity, what he is shaping in us through
all the struggles and suffering of our human existence. Our human
history has a goal; it is not a senseless turning in circles. Woven
through the whole fabric of things is a purpose that moves toward
a destination. And in Jesus Christ that purpose, that goal, that
destination, is revealed. That is a little of what it means that the
Word of God was made flesh.

James D. Smart, *The Recovery of Humanity*, pp. 21, 22

Among all gifts the gift of the Word of God is the most valuable.
For if you take this away, it is like taking the sun away from the
earth. For if the Word were removed, what would the world be but
a hell and a mere realm of Satan, though people of wealth, lawyers,
doctors, etc., dwelt in it? What can and do these people accomplish
without the Word? For only the Word keeps a joyful conscience,
a gracious God, and all of religion, since out of the Word, as from

a spring, flows our entire religion. Indeed, the Word sustains the entire world. Without the Word and Christ the world would not continue to exist for one moment. Therefore though there are many great gifts of God in the world, given for the benefit of man, yet the one gift which includes and sustains all the others is the Word, which proclaims that God is merciful and promises forgiveness of sins and life everlasting. But, I ask you, could this life still be considered life if we had to dispense with these blessings?

Ewald M. Plass, *What Luther Says*, Vol. III, p. 1,465

The Bible's concern is religious or theological. It wants to show what God is doing in and with history (redemption) rather than human causes and effects (politics, economics, etc.).

Moreover, the Bible was written in the ancient East, so its history cannot be expected to be "scientific" with modern science's nearly exclusive concern for facts and their secular relationships. It wants to state the *meaning* or the *truth of history* as seen under God. It is concerned with the experience of blessing and judgment at the hand of God. Accordingly, the biblical writers often arrange their material and use a poetic or non-literal approach in order to illustrate the truth (Genesis 8:11; Psalm 8:3). If God approved of such an approach by including it in our Bible, who are we to deny it and think that, if it is not scientific, it is not true?

This does not mean, however, that the Bible is unhistorical as we use the term. With due allowance for the difference between the "salvation-history" of the Bible and current definitions of secular history, archaeological and other discoveries have easily demonstrated the Bible's substantial accuracy. The time is past when skeptics and agnostics dare dismiss the Bible as a mere collection of pious legends and tales.

Theological Professors of The American Lutheran Church, *The Bible: Book of Faith*, p. 33

The idea is widespread that the Bible is a very simple book whose meaning should be evident, without any great effort, to anyone who cares to read it, and certainly without any extensive background of knowledge. Actually the Bible is a vast collection of ancient literature, composed by a host of authors over a period of more than twelve hundred years, in a world whose thought-forms were very different from ours. There are close to a million words in it. The amazing thing is that at so many points it speaks to us with such simplicity and directness and makes us feel that it was written specifically for us! And yet on every page it fairly bristles with problems and difficulties of interpretation. It yields its meaning only to patient, persistent study. It closes its doors to us when we become hurried and impatient.

James D. Smart, *The Rebirth of Ministry,* p. 76

Jesus Wrote with His Finger on the Ground [1]

Writing is made on stone, on leather,
    and on clay,
On paper spread afar to last
    for many a day.
Only the Word of God come down
    from heaven dare trust
His writing to the dust
That shall be swept away.

Writing is made by steel,
    by chisel, or by pen,
Or printed blackly down again
    and yet again.
Only the Word of God
    can be so very sure
His writing will endure,
Traced lightly by His finger
    on the hearts of men.

Edith Lovejoy Pierce, *The Christian Century,* July 16, 1958

[1] [See John 8:6.]

The simplicity—not ease—but simplicity of the Christian life is founded upon the fact of the presence of the Word of God already in the common life of the world. The practice of the Christian life consists of the discernment of (the seeing and hearing), and the reliance upon (the reckless and uncalculating dependence), and the celebration (the ready and spontaneous enjoyment) of the presence of the Word of God in the common life of the world. . . .

The experience of being a Christian is one of continually encountering in the ordinary and everyday events of life the same Word of God which is announced and heard, remembered and dramatized, expected and fulfilled in the sanctuary of the Church. To celebrate the Word of God in the sacramental worship of a congregation is an anticipation of the discernment of the same Word of God in the common life of the world. To be in the presence of the Word of God while in the world authenticates the practice of sacramental life within the congregation. One confirms and is confirmed by the other. In each place, in both world and Church, the Word is the same Word, and, in each place, in both practical life and sacramental life, the response elicited and the task required of the Christian is the same. . . .

The power to discern the Word of God is the mark of the Christian. It is not just one of an assortment of marks of the Christian; it is, in a sense, the unique mark essential to everything else which generally characterizes the Christian life. There can be no witness in the world to the Word of God by Christians individually or as the Church, save by the exercise of this power. There can be, of course, some witness to the Church, or to the churches, but neither of these is the same as the witness of Christians to the Word of God.

William Stringfellow, *A Private and Public Faith,* pp. 56, 57, 62

The Scripture meditation leads to prayer. We have already said that the most promising method of prayer is to allow oneself to be guided by the word of the Scriptures, to pray on the basis of a word of Scripture. In this way we shall not become the victims of our own emptiness. Prayer means nothing else but the readiness and willingness to receive and appropriate the Word, and, what is more, to accept it in one's personal situation, particular tasks, decisions, sins, and temptations. What can never enter the corporate prayer of the fellowship may here be silently made known to God. According to a word of Scripture we pray for the clarification of our day, for preservation from sin, for growth in sanctification, for faithfulness and strength in our work. And we may be certain that our prayer will be heard, because it is a response to God's Word and promise. Because God's Word has found its fulfillment in Jesus Christ, all prayers that we pray conforming to this Word are certainly heard and answered in Jesus Christ.

It is one of the particular difficulties of meditation that our thoughts are likely to wander and go their own way, toward other persons or to some events in our life. Much as this may distress and shame us again and again, we must not lose heart and become anxious, or even conclude that meditation is really not something for us. When this happens it is often a help not to snatch back our thoughts convulsively, but quite calmly to incorporate into our prayer the people and the events to which our thoughts keep straying and thus in all patience return to the starting point of the meditation.

Just as we relate our personal prayer to the Scripture passage so we do the same with our intercessions. It is impossible to mention in the intercessions of corporate worship all the persons who are committed to our care, or at any rate to do so in the way that is required of us. Every Christian has his own circle who have requested him to make intercession for them or for whom he knows he has been called upon especially to pray. These will be, first of all, those with whom he must live day by day.

This brings us to a point at which we hear the pulsing heart of all Christian life in unison. A Christian fellowship lives and exists by the intercession of its members for one another, or it collapses. I can no longer condemn or hate a brother for whom I pray, no matter how much trouble he causes me. His face, that hitherto may have been strange and intolerable to me, is transformed in intercession into the countenance of a brother for whom Christ died, the face of a forgiven sinner. This is a happy discovery for the Christian who begins to pray for others. There is no dislike, no personal tension, no estrangement that cannot be overcome by intercession as far as our side of it is concerned. Intercessory prayer is the purifying bath into which the individual and the fellowship must enter every day. The struggle we undergo with our brother in intercession may be a hard one, but that struggle has the promise that it will gain its goal.

Dietrich Bonhoeffer, *Life Together*, pp. 84–86

Hands hug.
What does it mean to clasp the hand
of another
and to say hello
and to say good-bye
and to say please and thank you
or to say
nothing at all?
What is the clasp of the hands
between two people,
where words fail
and where the common translation for the moment
is in the holding and gripping of the hands?
What is the intimate love and trust
beyond vocabulary and beyond spoken creeds
in the touching
and the clasping and grasping
and the gripping of hands, hugging
and wordless?
Hands have a language.
It was with the hands that Jesus
hugged the children
and the leper
and the blind man
and the lonely woman
and the loaves and the fishes
and the wood of the tree on the hill.
There is a spiritual language
that is neither Greek nor Hebrew nor Latin nor English
nor any spoken tongue,
with neither vowels nor consonants,
but is the flesh and blood
of one life gripping onto another
in love
and for love.
Holding hands is a sign
between people.

Herbert Brokering and Joseph Zimbolt, *Lifetimes*, p. 72

ESCHATOLOGY: THE HOPE
OF MANKIND

*The Christian faith looks forward in hope to the kingdom of God,
not backward to a golden age. The forward look is essential. If hope
is not at the center of the faith, it is not Christian or Biblical. Since
the beginning of our history, God has led His people forward
in hope.*

*What we hope for is the whole spectrum of good from now to
eternity. Our hope for life with God forever is not different from
our hope for peace and joy now — the kingdom of God on earth. It is
the same hope. We do not contrast the two aspects of hope. The
promise of eternal life has always been supported by a present hope
in this life; and we have always been strengthened against despair
in our hope for this world by the promise of eternity.*

We hope. We do not quarrel about the object of our hope.

Let us give thanks to the God and Father of our Lord Jesus
Christ! Because of His great mercy, He gave us new life by raising
Jesus Christ from the dead. This fills us with a living hope, and so
we look forward to possess the rich blessings that God keeps for his
people. He keeps them for you in heaven, where they cannot decay
or spoil or fade away. They are for you, who through faith are kept
safe by God's power, as you wait for the salvation which is ready
to be revealed at the end of time.

1 Peter 1:3-5, TEV

My dear friends, we are now God's children, but it is not yet
clear what we shall become. But this we know: when Christ appears,
we shall become like him, because we shall see him as he really is.

1 John 3:2, *Good News for Modern Man* (TEV)

Vast parts of the world believe in reincarnation. We die only to reappear. In most religions this belief is of no comfort. It hangs over people as a threat. The grim prospect is that men will be born again and again, each rebirth a punishment for the sins of the previous life.

It is not so with the Christian's hope. Christ, our Lord, arose from the dead. We, too, who are his shall also rise again. But we do not reappear in a life of new torments. We are promised a life forever free from sin, tragedy, and death. We are ushered into a life never again to die, and a life free from tears and pain, a life of endless joy with him.

This does not mean that we have balanced the books neatly in this life. We have not deserved a resurrection. Christ balanced the books for us. He took upon himself all our sins and the sins of the whole world. We need not fear punishment in a new incarnation, for the punishments have been erased forever by him who took upon himself our punishment.

The joy of Easter is not merely the promise of another life after this one. Many people would rather be extinguished like a flame than repeat the sort of years they have known. The joy of Easter lies primarily in knowing that it really was God who died for our sins on Good Friday and that, therefore, we have a right to live with God here and now and also hereafter forever. For our deepest need is for God himself. And Easter is the guarantee that we can have him again.

The Scriptures assure us, "Beloved, we are God's children now; it does not yet appear what we shall be, . . . but we shall be like him." We are God's children now because Jesus Christ lived, died, and arose again for our salvation. This opens a life for us which on the other side of death will be renewed into a life of unspeakable glory and joy.

Alvin Rogness, *Captured by Mystery*, p. 141

The great value of the doctrine of the Second Coming is that it guarantees that history is going somewhere. We cannot tell how it will happen, and when it will happen. We cannot take as literal truth the Jewish pictures of it which Paul used. We need not think of a physical coming of Christ in the clouds, or a physical trumpet blast. But what the doctrine of the Second Coming conserves is the tremendous fact that there is one divine, far-off event to which the whole creation is moving; there is a consummation; there is a final triumph of God. In his book, *An Arrow into the Air,* John H. Withers has a quotation, from Gerald Healy's play *The Black Stranger.* It comes from the days of the Irish potato famine in 1846. At that time as part of the relief work men were set to making roads which had no purpose whatever. It was simply to give them some work to do. One day in that desperate situation Michael comes home to his father, and says with a kind of poignant disillusionment: "They're makin' roads that lead to nowhere!" When we confess our ignorance, an ignorance which even Jesus shared, of dates and times; when we abandon all the Jewish imagery and pictures, which by this time have become only fantastic; when we strip the doctrine of the Second Coming down to its bare essentials; we are left with this tremendous truth—the Doctrine of the Second Coming is the final guarantee that life can never be a road that leads to nowhere; it is a road which leads to Christ.

William Barclay, *The Mind of St. Paul,* pp. 229, 230

Actually, it is remarkable how little emphasis the Bible puts upon the beyond or the future. We are not even to think about the "morrow," but rather leave it to God's care. We are to live *today,* in the here and now! And even when the Second Coming of the Lord is described, as for example in the Book of Revelation, the stress, amazingly, is not upon details of the life to come. On the contrary, its whole intent is to convey to the church in the *present* moment of her struggle this message: He who is the final victor will be king. And this king is Jesus Christ. You are not a poor little cult, cherishing a memory; you are a community of people who can lift up your heads because your Redeemer is drawing near from the other side. All of these pictures of the future are words of comfort and encouragement to battle for the church militant here and now, for its present hour of decision.

All one has to do is to compare the literature of that time with the New Testament and one will immediately see the difference between them. Outside the biblical literature a fantastic imagination produced great descriptions of the world to come, replete with detail. Comparing them, one is immediately struck by the holy restraint and temperateness of the Scriptures and their almost monotonous insistence that what matters is the *today* in which we hear his voice, and the *now* which is still the acceptable time. Even the account of the Ascension gives us no description of what things are like in the heaven to which Christ ascended, but is content with the terse statement that Christ is now sitting at the "right hand of God."

Helmut Thielicke, *Man in God's World*, p. 65

When my father died
I cried and cried
until I was weak.

After a while
I couldn't cry any more.
The tears wouldn't come.
Instead a strange hope
began to grow inside of me.

It was as if I were waking
from a very long sleep
and everything around me
had changed.

My father was still lying
in the casket.
He seemed to be waiting for me
to stop feeling sorry for myself
and to discover
what had happened to him.

Slowly,
as I looked at him,
my father was my father again.
All the crooked laughter lines
around his eyes
were as real as ever.

I realized then that
my father was living through death.
He was discovering the mystery of death
the way a child first discovers life.

He was enjoying
the birth pangs of a new life.

His first life
had been accepted
and sealed with death.

He was passing through the world of death
where Christ was at work
creating men for new tasks,
for new exciting worlds,
for new celebrations.

At that moment   God said, Yes,
Yes to death   and Yes to life.

The difference between life and death
seemed to vanish.
My father was alive in death,
and alive in me.
And God said, Yes! to me
that day.

Norman C. Habel, *For Mature Adults Only,* pp. 33, 34

debbie's song — And God Said, Yes!

1 And God said,   Yes!   Yes!   Yes!   Said
yes to the world once more, _____ Said
yes with a   cos - mic   roar, _____ Said
o - pen that   oth - er   door, _____ Said,
Yes,   yes,   yes, man!   Yes!   For God said

2 For God said, Yes! Yes! Yes!
  Let's splash the sky with light,
  Let's float the earth in space,
  Let's dance away the night,
  Said, Yes, yes, yes, man! Yes!

3 And God said, Yes! Yes! Yes!
  Let's make a man who's free,
  Creating life with love
  And ruling earth with Me.
  Said, Yes, yes, yes, man! Yes!

4 And God said, Yes! Yes! Yes!
  Let Jesus Christ be born!
  Let's find Him in the straw!
  Let's blast the shepherd's horn!
  Said, Yes, yes, yes, Son! Yes!

5 And God said, Yes! Yes! Yes!
  Yes to His broken Son!
  Yes to His open wound!
  Yes to the broken tomb!
  Said, Yes, yes, yes, Son! Yes!

6 And God said, Yes! Yes! Yes!
  We'll leap the swirling sky!
  We'll leap the hungry grave!
  We'll never stop to die!
  Said, Yes, yes, yes, man! Yes!

7 And God says, Yes! Yes! Yes!
  Says yes to that other door!
  Says yes when men say no!
  Says yes with a cosmic roar!
  Says, Yes, yes, yes, with me!

Norman C. Habel, *For Mature Adults Only*, p. 108

Christian faith not only affirms fully the reality of death but also looks upon death as an enemy to be overcome. Then it goes on to affirm that in the conflict between life and death the decisive battle has already been fought and won. This took place when Christ died and rose from the dead. Upon this one event, the resurrection of Christ, hinges the whole Christian message and the whole Christian hope. The divinity of Christ, the triumph of his mission, the restoration of man to fellowship with God, the beginning of the new creation, power for the transformation of life, the hope of life to come — everything that the church teaches obtains its validity and its vitality from the resurrection of Christ. "If Christ has not been raised, then our preaching is vain . . . and you are still in your sins" (1 Cor. 15:14 ff.) . . . .

The uniqueness of the Christian view sets it in sharp opposition to all forms of speculation about immortality. It is a view which is not derived from debating the legitimacy of human desires or the plausibility of an eventual realization of the potentialities of the human spirit. The solution takes place within the actual course of history. Jesus does more than remove the fear of death and set straight men's thinking about death. He conquers death itself. He died a real death and returns in triumph. He rises not as a disembodied spirit but with a resurrection body. That body is the evidence that the reign of death is over. Our hope for life after death does not consist in getting rid of our bodies and living on as souls. It is the assurance that the Spirit of God will transform "our lowly body to be like his glorious body" (Phil. 3:21).

T. A. Kantonen, *Life After Death*, pp. 29, 30

We used to think that one of the inalienable rights of man was that he should be able to plan both his professional and his private life. That is a thing of the past. The force of circumstances has brought us into a situation where we have to give up being "anxious about tomorrow" (Matt. 6:34). But it makes all the difference whether we accept this willingly and in faith (as the Sermon on the Mount intends), or under continual constraint. For most people, the compulsory abandonment of planning for the future means that they are forced back into living just for the moment, irresponsibly, frivolously, or resignedly; some few dream longingly of better times to come, and try to forget the present. We find both these courses

equally impossible, and there remains for us only the very narrow
way, often extremely difficult to find, of living every day as if it were
our last, yet living in faith and responsibility as though there were
to be a great future: "Houses and fields and vineyards shall again
be bought in this land," proclaims Jeremiah (32:15), in paradoxical
contrast to his prophecies of woe, just before destruction of the holy
city. It is a sign from God and a pledge of a fresh start and a great
future, just when all seems black. Thinking and acting for the sake
of the coming generation, but being ready to go any day without fear
or anxiety—that, in practice, is the spirit in which we are forced to
live. It is not easy to be brave and hold out, but it is imperative.

Dietrich Bonhoeffer, *Letters and Papers from Prison*, 1967 rev. ed., p. 15

When Magdalena was fourteen years old, she lay upon her
deathbed. Luther prayed, "O God, I love her so, but thy will be
done." And turning to her, *"Magdalenchen,* my little girl, you would
like to stay with your father here and you would be glad to go to
your Father in heaven?"
     And she said, "Yes, dear father, as God wills."
     And Luther reproached himself because God had blessed him
as no bishop had been blessed in a thousand years, and yet he could
not find it in his heart to give God thanks. Katie stood off, overcome
by grief; and Luther held the child in his arms as she passed on.
When she was laid away, he said, *"Du liebes Lenichen,* you will rise
and shine like the stars and the sun. How strange it is to know that
she is at peace and all is well, and yet to be so sorrowful!"

Roland H. Bainton, *Here I Stand*, p. 304

The Christian's view of death is different from that of the great
unbelieving mass of people in the world. Christians look at it as
a journey and departure out of this misery and vale of tears (where
the devil is prince and god) into yonder life, where there will be
inexpressible and glorious joy and eternal blessedness. Diligently
they study the art of looking at death in this way. Daily they
practice it, and earnestly they ask our dear Lord Christ to grant
them a blessed hour of departure and to comfort them in it with His
Spirit, that they may commit their soul to Him with true faith,
understanding, and confession. To such people death is not terrible

but sincerely welcome, especially in this last, dangerous time. For, as Scripture says, death takes them away before the calamity comes. They enter into peace and rest in their chambers (Is. 57:1-2).

Ewald M. Plass, *What Luther Says*, Vol. I, p. 382

I do not like to see people glad to die. I prefer to see them fear and tremble and turn pale before death but nevertheless pass through it. Great saints do not like to die. The fear of death is natural, for death is a penalty; therefore it is something sad. According to the spirit, one gladly dies; but according to the flesh, it is said: "Another shall carry thee whither thou wouldst not" (John 21:18).

Ewald M. Plass, *What Luther Says*, Vol. I, p. 368

We go along to the grave. We see that this person passes away today, that one tomorrow—persons with whom we have daily associated. Indeed, we know that death never skips or spares anybody and that no one ever returns. And yet we go on like the blind, who see as little at midday as in the pitch-dark night. We do not take these examples to heart; we do not realize that today or tomorrow our turn will come. So we keep our old habits, trot along at the same old pace, like old nags which refuse to have their gait changed by the whip.

Ewald M. Plass, *What Luther Says*, Vol. I, p. 365

O Lord, take us to tomorrow.
Give us trust.
Take away fear and trembling.
Take us beyond superstition.
Lead us in our life.
Be present in our daily history,
and through Christ help us see ordinary days
    as holy history.
May we not depend upon fate.
Rather lead us through the excitement
of not knowing for sure
what we need not know for certain.
We are grateful that we know
only what we need to know.
At least, O Lord, tell us for sure
what we can know for sure.
Tell us in Your Word
how You made ordinary events to be miraculous
    and made common people to be extraordinary.
Be near. Make sure, Holy Spirit.
Amen.

Herbert F. Brokering, *Lord Be With*, p. 139

Lord, we remember the dead;
we pray for those who mourn.
When we do not know what to say
or what to ask
and for what to pray,
comfort us.
Keep us talking to You
about those who are taken from our midst,
often to our great surprise and sorrow.
We know the feeling of those
who stood helplessly
when Jesus died.
Give to us the hope
those same people had
when Jesus arose.
Let us celebrate toward that day
when we shall all be united
and live.
In all our worship and contemplation
and all our sacred songs,
assure us of the community of all saints.
Spirit of God,
keep us united
through Him who arose.
Amen.

Herbert F. Brokering, *Lord Be With*, p. 145

Hope is one of the Theological virtues. This means that
a continual looking forward to the eternal world is not (as some
modern people think) a form of escapism or wishful thinking, but
one of the things a Christian is meant to do. It does not mean that
we are to leave the present world as it is. If you read history you
will find that the Christians who did most for the present world were
just those who thought most of the next. The Apostles themselves,
who set on foot the conversion of the Roman Empire, the great men
who built up the Middle Ages, the English Evangelicals who
abolished the Slave Trade, all left their mark on Earth, precisely
because their minds were occupied with Heaven. It is since
Christians have largely ceased to think of the other world that they
have become so ineffective in this. Aim at Heaven and you will get
earth "thrown in": aim at earth and you will get neither. It seems
a strange rule, but something like it can be seen at work in other
matters. Health is a great blessing, but the moment you make health

one of your main, direct objects you start becoming a crank and
imagining there is something wrong with you. You are only likely
to get health provided you want other things *more*—food, games,
work, fun, open air. In the same way, we shall never save
civilisation as long as civilisation is our main object. We must learn
to want something else even more. . . .

The Christian says, "Creatures are not born with desires unless
satisfaction for those desires exist. A baby feels hunger: well, there
is such a thing as food. A duckling wants to swim: well, there is
such a thing as water. Men feel sexual desire: well, there is such
a thing as sex. If I find in myself a desire which no experience in
this world can satisfy, the most probable explanation is that I was
made for another world. If none of my earthly pleasures satisfy it,
that does not prove that the universe is a fraud. Probably earthly
pleasures were never *meant* to satisfy it, but only to arouse it, to
suggest the real thing. If that is so, I must take care, on the one
hand, never to despise, or be unthankful for, these earthly blessings,
and on the other, never to mistake them for the something else of
which they are only a kind of copy, or echo, or mirage. I must keep
alive in myself the desire for my true country, which I shall not find
till after death; I must never let it get snowed under or turned aside;
I must make it the main object of life to press on to that other
country and to help others to do the same."

NOTE.—There is no need to be worried by facetious people who
try to make the Christian hope of "Heaven" ridiculous by saying
they don't want "to spend eternity playing harps." The answer to
such people is that if they cannot understand books written for
grown-ups, they should not talk about them. All the scriptural
imagery (harps, crowns, gold, etc.) is, of course, a merely symbolical
attempt to express the inexpressible. Musical instruments are
mentioned because for many people (not all) music is the thing
known in the present life which most strongly suggests ecstasy and
infinity. Crowns are mentioned to suggest the fact that those who
are united with God in eternity share His splendour and power and
joy. Gold is mentioned to suggest the timelessness of Heaven (gold
does not rust) and the preciousness of it. People who take these
symbols literally might as well think that when Christ told us to be
like doves, He meant that we were to lay eggs!

C. S. Lewis, *Christian Behaviour*, pp. 55, 56, 57, 58

SOME SCRIPTURE RELATING TO ESCHATOLOGY AND RESURRECTION:

Matthew 22:23-31	Question regarding man with seven wives.
John 11:23-25	I am the Resurrection and the Life.
John 14:1-7	In My Father's house are many rooms.
Romans 8	We are more than conquerors.
1 Corinthians 15	Christ has been raised from the dead.
2 Corinthians 5:1-10	If earthly tent is destroyed . . . we have a building from God.
Philippians 3:8-10	That I may know Him and the power of His resurrection.
1 Peter 1:3-9	We have been born anew to a living hope.

The celebration of Easter
is like a circus long overdue.
Easter is like one day when
all circuses come to one town
and the tents of God are packed with expectation,
overflowing with expectant people.
O that balloons would rise
and hands would clap
to the rhythmic cry for joy of all children.
Hosanna. Hosanna.
Blessed be God. Blessed be God.
In the midst of any circus tent
and tense crowd
there is the resemblance of a great act
performed once and for all people,
by which all crowds are brought face to face
with the living God.
It is the great event
rehearsed in the heavens,
performed first in Judaea,
and traveling continually on the road,
night and day,
through every large city
and every little place.
The act is named Redemption.
The great event is named Holy Week.
The performer is named the Father, the Son,
        and the Holy Spirit.
The audience is the whole world and all its people.

Herbert F. Brokering and Joseph Zimbolt, *Lifetimes,* p. 19

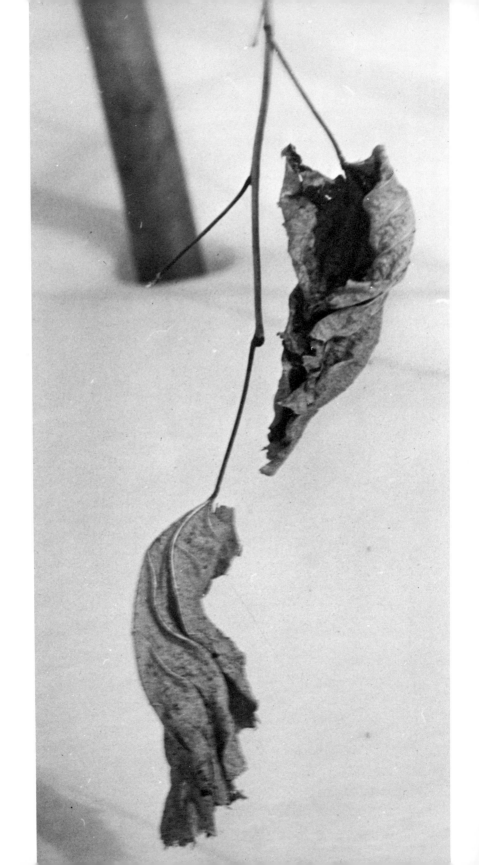

Dance, death!
Your deeds are done.
A new time has set in
and you are summoned by the Maker.
One day
death itself
will dance before the Lord.
The wind and breath of the Lord
will call for death,
and slowly
death will bring all limp life
and all brittle forms of death
to the judgment seat.
God will pronounce death
guilty,
will sentence death to death
and thus sentence to death tears,
crying,
hunger,
lonesomeness,
and disease.
Even now
there is enough evidence gathered against death
by those who live under the Spirit.
They build evidence
while they work
and while they wait
for the dance
and death of death.
The date has been set.
God knows the hour.

Herbert F. Brokering and Sister Noemi, *In Due Season,* p. 10

GOD'S CARE AND MAN'S RESPONSE

*All your thoughts about meaning in life and your own place in this
world end in the word "God." He is the meaning, the all.*

*You could start with the word "God," know what He is like,
and from that decide what your world and your life mean. If you
start with someone else's description, you are letting him tell you
what you are, what your world is, and what you ought to do. This
may be a way to real knowledge and faith, as you accept and
experience the truth of God. On the other hand, this has often been,
and may still be, the brainwashing path of an authoritarian culture.*

*You can start with yourself and your world. You can look at
the world carefully and know its needs and its joys. In includes
such things as the Bible, the people of God, and Jesus Christ. From
all that you may know what God is like, and respond with what He
calls you to do. On the other hand, this has often been, and may still
be, a path that leads us to division and conflict.*

*God is there. He is live with us and before us. We do not make
Him up or use Him for our own purposes. But we cannot picture
Him or know Him perfectly. We know only the evidences He has
given us. We listen to the witness of other men as lost as we are. We
study the truths of Jesus and His people. We come to Him as He
has called us, and we worship with our fellowmen because we must.
We need God.*

Christ is the visible likeness of the invisible God. He is the
first-born Son, superior to all created things. For by him God
created everything in heaven and on earth, the seen and unseen
things, including spiritual powers, lords, rulers, and authorities. God
created the whole universe through him and for him. He existed
before all things, and in union with him all things have their proper
place. He is the head of his body, the church; he is the source
of the body's life; he is the first-born Son who was raised from
death, in order that he alone might have the first place in all

things. For it was by God's own decision that the Son has in himself
the full nature of God. Through the Son, then, God decided to
bring the whole universe back to himself. God made peace through
his Son's death on the cross, and so brought back to himself all
things, both on earth and in heaven.

Colossians 1:15-20, TEV

You are the people of God; he loved you and chose you for his
own. Therefore, you must put on compassion, kindness, humility,
gentleness, and patience. Be helpful to one another, and forgive one
another, whenever any of you has a complaint against someone else.
You must forgive each other in the same way that the Lord has
forgiven you. And to all these add love, which binds all things
together in perfect unity. The peace that Christ gives is to be the
judge in your hearts; for to this peace God has called you together
in the one body. And be thankful. Christ's message, in all its
richness, must live in your hearts. Teach and instruct each other
with all wisdom. Sing psalms, hymns, and sacred songs; sing to God,
with thanksgiving in your hearts. Everything you do or say, then,
should be done in the name of the Lord Jesus, as you give thanks
through him to God the Father.

Colossians 3:12-17, TEV

I believe that God has created me
    and all that exists.
He has given me and still preserves
my body and soul with all their powers.

He provides me with food and clothing,
    home and family, daily work,
    and all I need from day to day.
God also protects me in time of danger
    and guards me from every evil.

All this He does out of fatherly and
    divine goodness and mercy,
    though I do not deserve it.
Therefore, I surely ought to thank and
    praise, serve and obey Him.
This is most certainly true.

The Small Catechism in Contemporary English

During the Reformation the towering question was, "How does a man return to God?" In our day for vast numbers of men the question is, "Is there a God to whom a man may return?" God is no longer taken for granted. In the past four centuries the ingenuity of man to uncover the secrets of the physical world has tended to edge God out to the borders of life. He no longer is in the center. For many he has disappeared altogether.

With God gone, man is at a loss for a center. What is existence about? What meaning does it have? Is survival its only goal? And is survival alone a goal meaningful enough to arouse the noblest aspirations of man?

Alvin Rogness, *Forgiveness and Confession,* pp. 16, 17

It is commonplace to say of modern man that he has lost God. The dimension of transcendence is gone. God threatens him no longer; it is his world that now overwhelms him. Once it was God who sent the rain and the sun; it was God who favored an army with victory; it was God who returned a man to health; it was God who punished him in his disobedience and rewarded him in his faithfulness.

It cannot be denied that God has drifted off to the edges of man's daily life and perhaps for many has disappeared altogether. But not without man's grief. An emptiness and loneliness have overtaken modern man. A vacuum yawns before him. He has longings and yearnings for something — he knows not what — something that will give meaning and completeness to life. This something is God. It would be reassuring to have a God who acts in history, who puts limits to man's self-destruction, who stands by to help manage this planet. Left alone, man yields to panic or paralysis,

or both. He can stand to be the copilot, but he cannot stand to be the pilot; he can stand to be a son of God, but he cannot stand to be on the throne.

Alvin Rogness, *Forgiveness and Confession*, pp. 24, 25

This is modern man — without God. He may strut in bravado. He may distract himself with endless analyses. He may plunge headlong toward his limited goals. He may capitulate into despair and nihilism. But lurking underneath the surface of his consciousness is a great sadness, a homesickness. He wants to find a home in this universe. He may not use the words of Job, "Oh, that I knew where I might find Him," but the cry is there. Man wants God.

Alvin Rogness, *Forgiveness and Confession*, p. 27

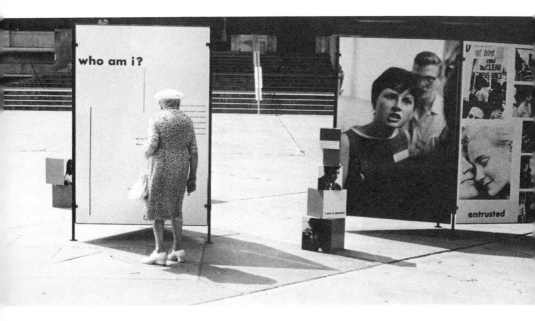

Tiger got to hunt,
Bird got to fly;
Man got to sit and wonder, "Why, why, why?"
Tiger got to sleep,
Bird got to land;
Man got to tell himself he understand.

Kurt Vonnegut Jr., *Cat's Cradle*, p. 124

With seven loaves of bread and a few small fish Jesus fed four thousand people, and still had seven baskets of food left over. This we call a miracle. Certainly it was unusual. But it is not only the unusual that is miraculous. It is usual for you to rise each morning with strength enough to put on your clothes and go to work. This is a repeating miracle each day. Your heart keeps pumping, your brain keeps ticking and your lungs keep breathing—all because an utterly strange power called *life* surges through you. It's the usual thing, but is a miracle nonetheless!

If your heart should falter and threaten to stop, and the doctor gives you only a 100 to 1 chance to live—and you pray—and health surges back like a tide—this you would call a miracle. This extraordinary turn toward health is, however, no greater a miracle than that your heart has kept pumping, seventy-two beats or more a minute, for fifty years.

Let us live each day in the wonder and awe of a Creator-Redeemer God who gives us life here and in his heavens hereafter forever!

With God nothing is impossible. This is the rock on which we live and work. The routine gifts given day by day are his work. The sun that shines and the rose that blooms are the wonder-works of his hands.

But there are greater miracles still, silent and unseen. He has created us to live with him. He has redeemed us in Christ to restore our rights to forgiveness and the eternal kingdom. Through such common things as words—in the Scriptures and in preaching—and such common elements as bread and wine in the Sacrament—he comes into our hearts to give us a new life and to reshape us for his kingdom.

Alvin Rogness, *Captured by Mystery*, pp. 38, 39

VIII

Listen to my opinion, accept or reject it.
The intellect is like a searchlight, it probes the darkness
    to and fro unceasingly,
Its rays at their limit describe a great sphere,
    and this is the universe of the intellect,
But this is not the universe of God, and God is not captured
    in it.
We do not search the darkness for Him, and pronounce that He
    is not there,
Nor do we hold Him caught in the beam, and declare Him to be
    exposed and humbled.
Our intellect is of finite glory, but God is of Infinite Glory;
It cannot make or unmake the Creator, it is He who created it.
It can rebel, but it is a proud and desolate rebellion;
We may yet fly to the stars, we may yet fire our guns and wake
    to echoing the waste mountains of long-dead places
But all that we do shall be of the order of what is done already,
    our searchlights fall back from the edge of the outermost void,
They fall back, they are exhausted, who shall make them rise
    higher?
Shall we say of the intellect, we shall devise means to exalt it?
Shall we say of our created nature, we shall otherwise create it?
No, we must say to the poets and to the humble, what moves in
    the outermost void?

IX

Do not pronounce judgment on the Infinite, nor suppose God to be
  like a bad Prime Minister
Do not suppose Him powerless, or if powerful malignant,
Do not address your mind to criticism of the Creator, do not pretend
  to know His categories,
Do not take His Universe in your hand, and point out its defects
  with condescension.
Do not think He is a greater potentate, a manner of President of
  the United Galaxies,
Do not think that because you know so few human beings, that He
  is in a comparable though more favorable position.
Do not think it absurd that He should know every sparrow, or the
  number of the hairs of your head,
Do not compare Him with yourself, not suppose your human love
  to be an example to shame Him.
He is not greater than Plato or Lincoln, nor superior to Shakespeare
  and Beethoven,
He is their God, their powers and their gifts proceeded from Him,
In infinite darkness they pored with their fingers over the first word
  of the Book of His Knowledge.

X

This is not reason, men do call it faith.
If ten men came to me, now some I should confound, and by some
 be confounded,
And those I do confound shall leave me for an easier victory
And those that me confounded shall find elsewhere defeat.
And who, to God found in an argument, will put out supplicating
 hands?
I do not lie to you, I tell you plainly,
I do not presume to bring my knowledge into His presence,
 I go there humbly
All this I recommend to you, it is the heart of worship.

Alan Paton, "Meditation for a Young Boy Confirmed"
The Christian Century, Oct. 13, 1954, p. 1,238

There is prevalent among us Christians a manner of speech that manifests itself every time something terrible happens to us; it occurs, for example, in many death notices. "God, the Almighty, has taken away our son. God has visited cancer upon me. God has sent loneliness upon me." The idea back of all these expressions is that it is *God* who sends all these terrible things upon us: he not only creates the blossoms, but also the frost that blights them. He not only creates infants, but he also sends infantile paralysis upon them.

This is an utterly and completely unbiblical idea. On the contrary, what we hear in the Bible again and again is that the powers of sin and suffering and death are *hostile* powers, enemies of God. God did *not* will that they should exist. They are disorderly and unnatural powers which broke into God's plan of creation. They are the dark henchmen of original sin, our *own* sin. And just because these powers are hostile powers, Jesus' struggle against them often took on dramatic form. At the grave of his friend Lazarus, Jesus wept tears of mingled anger and sorrow. His spirit was angered by the dark powers that snatched away his friend and was grieved that these powers should be able to break into God's world since man through his fall has opened the door for them. And in the healing of the paralytic, Jesus again makes it very plain that the sickness which he healed is only the other side of the same derangement and disorder which sin brought into the world. All these things are signs of the disorder, the rift that runs through the midst of creation.

Helmut Thielicke, *Our Heavenly Father*, pp. 24, 25

God is not *identical* with his creatures, not identical with the world, and even though they all came from his hand, even though he clothes the lilies of the field and feeds the birds of the air, even though we can say "Our Father" to him, God nevertheless stands at a *distance* from all these things and from all of us. We must say to him: We are sinners, but thou art the Holy One; we are the accused, but thou art the Judge; we are under the dominion of guilt and tears and death, but thy kingdom is not of this world! And when one day that kingdom comes, there will be no more suffering nor crying nor death any more, and every tear will be wiped away from our eyes — so "different," so "otherworldly" is thy kingdom!

That is the Bible's conception of the world beyond. God is not simply identical with the world, he is not merely "the inmost force which binds the world together." He is not merely another word for generative life and the harmony of its laws. God is the "wholly Other," the Creator who is at the same time strictly separate from his creatures and will not suffer them to intrude upon his sphere, as man does when he makes himself God. He is the "totally Other," the Holy One who is strictly divorced from sin. "Depart from me, for I am a sinful man, O Lord." This is what the Bible means by a God who is outside and beyond the world.

Helmut Thielicke, *Man in God's World,* pp. 69, 70

Lord,
You have made and given us
    sunshine, the snow,
    the rain, and the sunset.
You have created a world of season,
    rhythms, moods,
    a world of sunrises and eclipses,
    incoming and outgoing tides,
    cold fronts and heat waves.
For calendars and skywatching
You have given to man the exact time
    for the eclipse,
    for the tide and sunset,
    for full moon and for leap year.
Make man the guardian and keeper
    of the days and nights,
    of the winters and springs,
        the flurries and torrents,
        the waves and the winds.
Make us glad for earth's rhythm and rhyme,
in which we were born to laugh and cry,
    live and die and rise.

Fix our hearts on Christ,
the First fruit of all creation. [1]
Amen

Herbert F. Brokering, *Lord, Be With*, p. 61

[1] [The children of Israel were commanded to bring the first fruits of their harvest as a gift to God, to show that the whole harvest was God's. Jesus is the Firstfruit of creation: His resurrection means that all men will rise from the dead. See 1 Cor. 15:20.]

One reads the Bible to learn about what God has done in the past to redeem his people and his world. As one reads, there emerges a pattern, a shape, a style, a fairly consistent way of doing things and of reacting to situations. There are many pictures, or word-images, in the Bible which describe this way — covenant, law, love, justification, forgiveness, sanctification, kingdom of God, resurrection — the list could be extended indefinitely. A valid reading of the Bible will take all of these images seriously because all contribute to a grasp of God's way with his world. The word "redemption" has been singled out here simply because it suggests nicely both the need for redemption and the possibility for redemption. The word implies both the "accidentally evil" and the "substantially good" which we have seen to be basic to the Christian's posture toward the world in which he lives. There is no thought here that "God's way" is completely simple and obvious. Particularly in the Old Testament, God frequently changes his tactics. He "repents." He demonstrates all the versatility of a broken-field runner in a football game. He zigs and he zags. Yet there is relentless consistency, a clear passion to finish the task of reconciling the whole creation to himself, of bringing it back to its original purpose, of redeeming it.

Harvey Cox quotes Archie Hargraves of the Urban Training Center in Chicago, as saying that the church is something like a floating crap game in which the Christian can be compared to a gambler who never knows for certain just what is going to happen. He lives his life in constant risk — or "faith." But he asks the question, "Where's the action?" and he goes where the action is. That is, he tries to get in on what God is doing.

There are enormous risks in this way of reading the world and of phrasing the ethical question. But as Joseph Sittler says, "the risk belongs to the glory." God took an incalculable risk when he created man to be a responsible creature. But even though this creature has misused his responsibility, would God — or would you — want it any other way? God is not a puppeteer, but a choreographer. He doesn't just pull strings. He stands in the wings, directing the action. He doesn't run out on the stage every time a dancer stumbles or an actor blows a line. As long as the curtain is open, the show goes on. There are enormous risks. And there are disastrous mistakes. But God never abandons his creation. The church lives in the Scriptures and in constant conversation with the saints of all ages, in order to learn God's way and, hopefully and faithfully, to get in on his action in the world.

James H. Burtness, *Whatever You Do,* pp. 86 – 88

When now they were come to Bethlehem, the Evangelist says that they were, of all, the lowest and the most despised, and must make way for everyone until they were shoved into a stable to make a common lodging and table with the cattle, while many cutthroats lounged like lords in the inn. They did not recognize what God was doing in the stable. With all their eating, drinking, and finery, God left them empty, and this comfort and treasure was hidden from them. Oh, what a dark night it was in Bethlehem that this light should not have been seen. Thus God shows that he has no regard for what the world is and has and does. And the world shows that it does not know or consider what God is and has and does.

Joseph had to do his best, and it may well be that he asked some maid to fetch water or something else, but we do not read that anyone came to help. They heard that a young wife was lying in a cow stall and no one gave heed. Shame on you, wretched Bethlehem! The inn ought to have been burned with brimstone, for even though Mary had been a beggar maid or unwed, anybody at such a time should have been glad to give her a hand.

There are many of you in this congregation who think to yourselves: "If only I had been there! How quick I would have been to help the Baby! I would have washed his linen. How happy I would have been to go with the shepherds to see the Lord lying in the manger!" Yes, you would! You say that because you know how great Christ is, but if you had been there at that time you would have done no better than the people of Bethlehem. Childish and silly thoughts are these! Why don't you do it now? You have Christ in your neighbor. You ought to serve him, for what you do to your neighbor in need you do to the Lord Christ himself.

Roland H. Bainton, *The Martin Luther Christmas Book,* pp. 37, 38

Catch it
before it disappears.
It is round like the world,
and it is fun,
but it will disappear.
Heaven and earth will pass away.
It is made by the Word of the Lord,
but the Word of the Lord will live forever.
The earth is more than a soap ball
filled with the skillful breath of a man
with a bubble pipe in hand.
It is a ball of dust and water
and seas and creeping things,
fishes of the water, fowl of the air,
beast and man;
and it is made by the gigantic breath of God
with eternity in His lips.
When He had made the earth,
God made man
and gave him to the earth.
It is round like a bubble,
and it is fun,
and it will disappear.
Take it, all men, women and children,
for it has not yet disappeared.
It is fun!
The fullness of the Lord is upon it.
Be glad.

Herbert F. Brokering and Joseph Zimbolt, *Lifetimes,* p. 6

Clothe the naked and you clothe Jesus.
That's what Jesus said.
It is the poor
who summon the world before the justice of Jesus.
The distance to Jesus
is the distance to tattered clothing,
rips, knots, holes, shreds,
and to the look — Clothe me.
Jesus said, the distance
to the kingdom called heaven
can be measured by nakedness, loneliness, hunger,
and thirst.
The closeness
to the Kingdom
is measured by clothing the poor,
visiting the lonely,
feeding and quenching the hungry and thirsty.
To see
the one in tatters and rips
is but part of the secret.
The more powerful part of the secret
is to be there and
to be seen
by the child in tatters and in need.

Herbert F. Brokering and Joseph Zimbolt, *Lifetimes*, p. 38

HISTORY OF THE PEOPLE OF GOD: A Synopsis

The Bible is an amazing collection of books. It deals with thousands of years of human history. It finds the meaning of that history in God's action to save His people. It promises the coming of God's kingdom of peace. Admittedly, this is a bold claim.

You cannot say that the Bible is true or untrue, or that it is an important book, unless you make a thorough study of it. This is not easy, however. The sheer size of the Bible can be discouraging, to say nothing of the fact that it is written in a variety of styles, or that it reflects cultures and customs which are foreign to us. It is not a secret or mysterious book, but a little help in studying it is almost necessary. The following brief survey of the Bible is intended to give you that help. Since it is so sketchy, it is bound to be incomplete to the point of distortion. It is not meant to replace your own reading of the Bible.

Most books have an introduction. The Bible is no exception. Its opening chapters suggest the major themes and the key issues. Genesis 1 — 11 introduces the main characters, God and man, and gives a picture of what their relationship ought to be and what it actually is. Think of these chapters as stories about God and you — who you are, what you might be, who God is, and what He will do. When you see the introduction this way, you can read the whole Bible as personally addressed to you.

Genesis 1:26
Image of God

The opening phrase sets the stage for the whole book. "In the beginning God . . . ." God is the beginning of everything. Nothing exists all by itself. It has a meaning, a place as part of an intended whole. The Creator of all that exists is God, and man is made in His image. He is made to belong to God, communicate

Genesis 2:18-25
Community

with Him, and live in a love relationship with Him. Even the fact that man cannot live in isolation but establishes family and community ties is part of God's meaning for us.

Genesis 3
Nature of Sin

Genesis 3 gives a graphic picture of the major human problem. Man chooses to control his life and destiny by the knowledge of good and evil. He makes the choice knowing that before God that choice is death. He does not choose life. This is called sin. The promise of the Tempter, "You will be like God" (Genesis 3:5), has great appeal to the human ego. The result of man's rebellion against God is guilt, fear, the tendency to deny responsibility, and finally death; that is separation from God.

Genesis 4:1-10
Murder

In a series of stories recorded in Genesis 4 — 11 the Biblical writers draw vivid pictures of human behavior. Jealousy caused brother to rise up against brother, and Cain killed Abel. Civilization, which man developed, did not stop the evil in man's heart. His self-assertion

Genesis 6 — 10
A New Start

reached such depths that God had to begin again. He sent a flood to save man — in Noah and his family — from the evil results of pride.

Still, the Bible tells us, man does not learn. The prologue concludes with an account of the building of the tower of Babel, another attempt on the part of man to "make a name for himself" (Genesis 11:4). His attempt to make himself the measure of greatness resulted only in division and anger.

When we see the persistent perversity of man we are tempted to say with Martin Luther,

"If I were God, I would have kicked the world to pieces long ago." But this is how God and man are different. Running through these opening chapters of Genesis is a theme which becomes more and more prominent until it climaxes in the story of Jesus Christ. It is the theme of God's unlimited love. Here are some of the examples of it. The man and the woman were driven from the Garden of Eden but not before they were given hope that the battle between the powers of evil and man would go on. Satan had not won the final victory (Genesis 3:15). Cain, the murderer, was preserved by a mark given by God. Noah and his family were saved in an ark which God instructed him to build.

God does not abandon people, even after they have turned away from Him. He tries again and again to win them back so they can realize the full purpose and joy of life. The story of God's love, or grace as it is often called, is the major theme of the Bible. God's demonstration of His saving love and man's response make up the remainder of the Biblical story.

Genesis 12
Abraham's Call

Ethnically God's people were known as Hebrews or Israelites. Their history began when God spoke to a man named Abraham and asked him to go to a new land to establish a new people. "Go from your country and your kindred and your father's house to the land that I will show you. And I will make of you a great nation and I will bless you and make your name great, so that you will be a blessing" (Genesis 12:1-2). In this covenant God called Abraham and all his descendants to be faithful to Him. He would give them His blessing which they in turn could pass on to others. "Blessed to be a blessing" is a summary way to state this important idea.

At about the year 2000 B. C. God began

a new pattern on earth. He called a particular
people out of the culture of their day to be His
representative on earth, that through them all
nations might come to know Him. They were
not called because He cared more about them
than about others, but because He cared for
all men. The covenant, or agreement, that He
made with them was His way of addressing
Himself to all men. They had a specific task.
They were a kind of working committee for
the benefit of all men. From Genesis 12 on,
the Old Testament is the record of this special
people. It shows their strengths and their failures,
God's continuing correction, forgiveness, and
salvation. God declared Himself to them so
that the world might know by their history and
their words what He is like.

The pattern has not changed. Two thousand
years later Peter wrote to all Christians, quoting
from the Old Testament to describe their new
covenant task for God: "You are a chosen race,
a royal priesthood, a holy nation, God's own
people, that you may declare the wonderful
deeds of Him who called you out of darkness
into His marvelous light" (1 Peter 2:9). The
history you read here may involve you. Joining
a church means being one of God's working
people, and this history is about your ancestors
in the faith.

It took faith on the part of Abraham to
act as he did. He had already moved with his
father from Ur to Haran. Now he left Haran
with his wife, Sarah, and nephew, Lot, and
traveled south to Canaan (Palestine). He
believed God would keep his promise that he
would be the father of a great nation, though
he was 75 years old, his wife was far past
childbearing age, and they had no children.

Genesis 21:1-7
Birth of Isaac

God did keep his promise. A son was born
and they named him Isaac. Circumcision of
all males was established as the outward sign

of God's covenant. It served as a constant
reminder — a sign engraved in the flesh — that
they were a covenant people with a special
task to perform for God.

Genesis 22:1-19
Abraham's Test

At each change in Abraham's family life
the covenant was repeated. God was calling
not just Abraham, but the nation which would
follow him, to faithfulness. When Lot left him,
when his first son by Hagar, his maid, was
rejected, and when Isaac was born, the covenant
was renewed. In a final test Abraham was
asked to sacrifice his son and then restrained —
to know that the covenant continued in Isaac.
Through such tests the generations which
followed produced a heritage of faith. They
became aware of their unique relationship to
God and their own identity as a people.

Genesis 25:24-34
Esau and Jacob

Genesis 32:22-30
Jacob Becomes Israel

Isaac grew up, married a woman by the
name of Rebekah, and they had twins named
Esau and Jacob. Jacob was chosen to carry on
the covenant responsibilities. After an all-night
struggle with God at a crisis in his life, his
name was changed to Israel, a name he
bequeathed to his descendants.

Jacob had 12 sons, fathers of the 12 tribes
of the nation of Israel. The older sons resented
the younger Joseph. When the opportunity
arose, they sold him as a slave to some traders
on their way to Egypt. After years of hardship,
including a few years in prison, Joseph became
a prominent man in Egyptian government and
brought his family to live with him. The origins
of Israel as a nation are therefore in Egypt.
God had brought them there for His own
purpose with them. Joseph's forgiveness of his
brothers indicates God's plan: "You meant
evil against me; but God meant it for good."
(Genesis 50:20)

The people grew to great numbers in Egypt.
A new dynasty came to the throne of Egypt,

and the Pharaohs feared the power of the Hebrews. Persecution began. But God did not forget His promise. Israel had been called to be a blessing to the nations. In Israel God was to show Himself again and again as a God of redemption, liberation, and freedom.

Exodus

God had not promised that the job would be easy. Life became hard for the Hebrews. They were used as slaves to build the great cities of Egypt. Although they were the oppressed people, the Egyptians feared them. In an attempt to control their population growth, an order was given that every male child should be killed at birth.

Exodus 2
Birth of Moses

A boy named Moses was saved from this fate when his mother hid him in a basket-like boat in the river. He was found and adopted by the Pharaoh's daughter, who hired his own mother as a nursemaid and governess. So Moses received both the best education available in Egypt and a knowledge of the heritage of his people. From his mother he heard about the covenant God had made with Abraham: that Israel was to have its own land and be a blessing to all nations. But this did not complete his education. In his eagerness to help as a young man, he killed an Egyptian who was beating one of his countrymen. To his surprise his own people did not appreciate his intervention, so he fled into the wilderness of the Sinai Peninsula. In the land of Midian he settled down, married, and became a sheephearder for his father-in-law. Moses came to know the desert country well.

Exodus 2
Moses Flees

Exodus 3
Moses' Call

The time was right. God heard His people cry for help and remembered His covenant with them. Under the symbol of a bush that burned but was not consumed, Moses heard the call of God to go and set His people free.

At first Moses refused. "Who am I that I should go to Pharaoh and bring the sons of Israel out of Egypt?" (Exodus 3:11). Finally after God disarmed him of his excuses and promised to support him, he agreed to go.

Exodus 12
Escape

Israel's escape from Egypt is known as the Exodus. It took place some 400 years after Joseph had brought his family to Egypt. A series of ten natural catastrophes fell on Egypt at Moses' call. In the last of them, the firstborn of all Egyptians, both man and animal, died. Israel was protected. The angel of death passed over their houses, their door posts having been streaked with the blood of a lamb while they ate their feast of freedom — the Passover meal — inside.

Exodus 14
The Red Sea

Pharaoh was reluctant to lose a nation of slaves. But he finally agreed to let them go with their flocks and a great deal of borrowed jewelry — into the desert for a weekend to worship their God, Moses said. Pharaoh probably knew that freedom was their objective, and pursued them with his army. Israel was again delivered by God's intervention at the Read Sea.

The exodus is a key event in Israel's history. It is the mighty act of deliverance by which God saved His people from bondage. God is still known among them — and among Christians — as "He who brought us up out of the land of Egypt." The Passover festival is still celebrated each spring by the Jewish people, and its concept of freedom is at the heart of the Christian Sacrament of the Altar, instituted by Jesus at the Passover meal.

Exodus 19 – 20
Covenant and the
Ten Commandments

God led the band of ex-slaves to Mount Sinai in the wilderness. There He renewed with the nation the covenant He had made with Abraham. He would be their God and bless them, and they would represent Him — and only

Him—among the nations. They were not to picture Him in any way, for God is a Mystery who always keeps the initiative for His own actions. And if Israel took His name and called themselves His people, He would hold them to their covenant. They could not take His name in vain. The freedom God gave to them they were to live out among themselves—in parental obedience, without killing, stealing, violating marriages, lying, or coveting. The Ten Commandments are Israel's place in the covenant, summarized in love for both God and man.

Deuteronomy 6:4-9
The Great
Commandment

The United Kingdom

Deuteronomy 27:9-10
Promise and Law

The people spent about 40 years in the wilderness, becoming a nation conscious of the presence and power of God. They entered the land originally promised to Abraham. Moses had died, and Joshua replaced him as their leader. They crossed the Jordan River, conquered a number of cities, and settled down in various areas of the land called Canaan. For several hundred years Israel was a loosely organized group of clans united mainly by their common faith in God. Leaders, called Judges, took over whenever the need arose. Men like Gideon and Jephthah led the people to victory over their enemies, but they did not unify the clans under one government.

Deuteronomy 34:9
Joshua Is Leader

1 Samuel 10:1
Saul Made King

However, as the threat of domination by a people known as Philistines grew, the people saw the advantages of a unified nation. So they demanded a king. Some leaders (particularly Samuel, priest and last of the Judges) were opposed to a monarchy. They feared that trust in God would be replaced by trust in a human leader. Samuel warned that a king would oppress them and pervert the concept of the people. However, under God's direction he anointed Saul as Israel's first king.

1 Samuel 31:1-7
Death of Saul

Saul was able to break the Philistine grip. But Samuel rejected him as king, and Saul himself proved to be emotionally unfit for the office. He committed suicide on the battlefield, and the Philistines gained control.

2 Samuel 5:1-4
David Made King

The man who followed Saul as king not only saved the nation from total defeat but brought his people to unsurpassed heights of glory. His name was David and he produced Israel's "golden age." He pushed back the enemies and expanded the borders of the nation. He established a new capital at Jerusalem and made Israel a great nation. Literature and music flourished. Material prosperity abounded. It seemed to the people ca. 1000 B. C. that God had completely fulfilled His promise. Abraham's descendants had become a great nation and the kingdom had been established. Centuries later, when the people looked for a "messiah," an anointed one to come, they expected him to be a "son of David."

David was a great man. As a leader and military strategist he stood far above his contemporaries. The psalms he composed reveal him as a man of deep faith. But David fulfilled the prophecy of Samuel. The kingdom was established with murder and civil war, and it was maintained only by military force. Heavy taxes were imposed, tribal leadership was ignored, worship was centralized and regulated, prophet and priest alike became servants of the king. The Bible is not a book about great heroes, but about a gracious God working with people as He finds them, calling them to reunion with Himself and forgiving them.

The Divided Kingdom

While Israel was at her height of prosperity, culture, and power the seeds of decay were sown. In the comfort of her security she forgot her purpose. All was going well. What more did she need? The people were grateful for "God's blessings," but the call to be a blessing to others was nearly forgotten.

1 Kings 1:28-40
Solomon Made King

It was not that the people were irreligious! In fact ritual flourished. During the reign of Solomon, David's son, a magnificent temple

1 Kings 6:1-38
Temple Is Built

was built. Religious pilgrimages were made, and the splendor of the temple and its rites were dedicated to God. A visitor to the land could not have accused the people of lack of religion, yet the Biblical historians make it clear that this was the beginning of Israel's fall.

1 Kings 9:15-22
Forced Labor

Solomon ruled from about 960 B. C. to 925 B. C. The unprecedented prosperity of his reign was tainted by the higher and higher taxation and the drafting of citizens into work battalions needed to maintain the government building programs. Outwardly the time was characterized by progress in art, literature, music, wealth, religion, and national security, but Israel had lost sight of her God-given assignment and she was doomed.

1 Kings 12:1-16
Rebellion

When Solomon died around 925 B. C., rebellion flared up, and the nation was divided. Civil war broke out, and the nation was never again united. The northern area retained the name Israel, and the south was called Judah, although the name Israel often referred to the whole area as it does today. The next three or four centuries of the history of God's people present a complex and sad picture. Not only were they divided as a nation, but the succession of kings in both sections produced very few noble leaders.

In addition to the political confusion, the religious life deteriorated. The pagan fertility cults of Canaan were easily mixed with the worship of God. It became apparent that David's empire had succeeded at a time of weakness in the surrounding powers. Kings

like Ahab strove to maintain power through
military alliances with other nations. Israel's
status as a people peculiar to God was
compromised. As in the days of the judges,
God gave leaders when leaders were needed.
He called His prophets to oppose both the
kings and their hired priests and prophets.
Elijah, first of the great prophets, challenged
the people: "How long will you go limping
with two different opinions? If the Lord is
God, follow Him; but if Baal, then follow him."
(1 Kings 18:21)

There were a number of attempts to reform
both the political and religious life of Israel
and Judah, but none had lasting effects.
Apparently the people were too divided, too
concerned about material prosperity, too
unaware of their purpose to survive.

2 Kings 25:7
Fall of Jerusalem

The northern province fell to the Assyrians
in 721 B. C. and disappeared as a nation. The
south hung on for over a century but in 586
B. C. it too crumbled before the Babylonian
onslaught.

The Exile

In three successive attacks the Babylonians
took the best of the Hebrew people to their
land. So Judah, the land of promise, was in
ruins, and the survivors were captives. In
exile, away from their land and their religious
center, they wondered if they could survive
as a people. Many were disillusioned. "By the
waters of Babylon, there we sat down and wept
when we remembered Zion." (Psalm 137:1)

Two prophets — Jeremiah in Jerusalem and
Ezekiel in Babylon — held Israel to her covenant
promise. Through them God reminded His
people that He was not bound to a nation,
a land, or a temple. The kingdom of power had
been a mistake — destroyed to return the people
to their covenant purpose.

The Prophets

The books of the prophets are separated in our Bible from the record of Israel's history. Yet they are the most important voices in the Old Testament and the most powerful shapers and interpreters of that history. Nearly all of them were called by God from outside the "establishment," to speak as rebels and critics against it. They were known as men who spoke for God, yet they were nearly always lonely, hated, and feared. They were preachers in the marketplace, poets and orators; their words were gathered and compiled only years after they spoke, when Israel realized that they had been right in what they said.

In times of prosperity they called the people to repentance, promising hope in God only if they remembered the covenant and lived before God in justice, love, and freedom. Amos the shepherd saw the evils of the city's commerce and the hollowness of its ritual. Hosea realized in his faithless wife the constant love of God to faithless Israel. The early Isaiah wept at the folly of the people frantic for power and wealth. They accused the political leaders of being false to the covenant, and the religious leaders of misleading a people weak and without understanding. Finally, when Israel refused to repent, Jeremiah and Ezekiel preached the destruction of the kingdom without any hope.

When Jerusalem and the temple were destroyed and Israel had no hope in herself, Ezekiel, Jeremiah, and Isaiah spoke of the hope in the covenant. God had chosen this people. His purposes were expressed in Israel's history, and He would yet restore her to faithfulness. The people's future lay not in power and wealth but in God alone.

They spoke for God with words such as, "Behold, the days are coming, says the Lord, when I will make a new covenant with the

house of Israel and the house of Judah"
(Jeremiah 31:31). "I, I am He who blots out
your transgressions for My own sake, and
I will not remember your sins" (Isaiah 43:25).
"I am the Lord, I have called you in
righteousness, I have taken you by the hand
and kept you; I have given you as a covenant
to the people. A light to the nations, to open
the eyes that are blind, to bring out the
prisoners from the dungeon, from the prison
those who sit in darkness." (Isaiah 42:6, 7)

For a thousand years, through the exile,
the message of the prophets led the people of
Israel—judgment where they had missed their
mission and hope when they realized they had
failed. Judgment and hope stood side by side
because God brough them both.

Isaiah 42:1-4,
52:13—53:12
Servant Poems

One important concept was part of the
heritage of the people from the beginning and
was amplified by Isaiah. It was the concept of
the servant. Although the word was not used,
the call to Abraham and his descendants implied
that the people were to be servants of God.
Isaiah understood in the destruction of
Jerusalem that being a servant included
suffering under the burden of all men. Later,
Jesus became the example and fulfillment of
Isaiah's words, Israel's mission: "But He was
wounded for our transgressions, He was
bruised for our iniquities; upon Him was the
chastisement that made us whole, and with
His stripes we are healed. All we like sheep
have gone astray; we have turned every one
to his own way; and the Lord has laid on Him
the iniquity of us all." (Isaiah 53:5, 6)

The suffering servant motif continues for
the people of God today. We are called by
Old Testament prophets and New Testament
apostles to be the suffering servant, patterned
after Christ. God's plan and mode of operation
have been consistent down through the years.

The Bible is not simply ancient history. Through it God still leads us today.

The Return

The people of Israel had lost sight of their purpose. They had lived for themselves and trusted in their own strength. They had lost their land and their identity as a nation. Most of them were exiled to Babylon.

Their period of captivity lasted approximately 70 years. About 520 B. C. Persia conquered Babylon and a "new exodus" took place. Some of the Hebrew people in Babylon returned to Palestine. Under the leadership of Nehemiah the walls of Jerusalem were rebuilt in roughly 440 B. C. A little later Ezra drastically reformed the worship and cultic life of the people.

The people of God in Jerusalem were few and very poor. The temple was small, times were hard, and surrounding people were hostile. Many Jews had moved to all parts of the world during the exile. Jerusalem became a spiritual center of a scattered people, rather than the political capital of a nation. In their poverty and because of the exile, they tended to become fanatically faithful to the letter of the covenant: sterile observance of the laws of worship.

Between the Testaments

During this period the Hebrew canon of sacred books became fixed, and the record of the Old Testament ends. But the history of God's people continued during the 400 years before Christ was born. Persia, which had been the major power, fell, and Alexander the Great of Macedonia swept across the Mediterranean world in about 325 B. C. He and his armies imposed the influence of Greek culture on the known world. After his death

the empire was divided among four generals.
Since Palestine controlled major trade routes
to the east, the Seleucid kings in Damascus
and the Ptolemaic kings in Egypt fought for
control. The Seleucid kings won, and attempted
to force the Jews into the Greek way of life.
A major rebellion led by the Maccabees around
165 B. C. succeeded, even though it became
as much a civil war against Hellenistic Jews
as a war of freedom from Damascus.

Within a few generations Maccabean
leadership collapsed in a sordid family battle
for power. Rome was called in to establish
order, and in 63 B. C. Jerusalem was besieged
and sacked by Pompey. Palestine became
a province of Rome, a vassal kingdom under
the Herods. The time was right for God's act
of redemption in Jesus Christ. The known
world was united under one government, tied
together by a network of roads and equipped
with one universal language, Greek. The
possibilities for travel and communication were
the best they had ever been or would be for
many centuries to come. Religiously too, the
world seemed poised, waiting for something
new to break into human history. The time
had fully come!

The Life of Jesus the Christ

The story of Jesus has been given to us by four Biblical writers. While they duplicate each other in many ways, each of the four gospels offers a distinctive portrait of Jesus. Matthew, Mark, Luke, and John were interested in presenting not only historical facts but the meaning of Jesus' life. Through them God reveals Himself to us.

The Birth of Jesus

Matthew 1:18-25
Luke 2:1-20
Birth of Jesus

Only Matthew and Luke record the birth of Jesus. Both of them indicate that His birth was extraordinary. They reflect the conviction of those who knew Him that Jesus was not only completely a man, born like every other baby, but that in Him God was present among us.

Very little is known of Jesus' childhood. After His birth in Bethlehem his parents fled to Egypt for a time to escape the wrath of a jealous Herod. Most of His life, until He began His ministry, was spent in Nazareth. The only other incident from His childhood recorded by Luke tells of a pilgrimage to Jerusalem at the age of 12.

Luke 2:41-52
Jesus in Jerusalem

Baptism and Temptation

Mark, perhaps the first gospel to be written, begins with Jesus' baptism by John the Baptizer. Immediately after this Jesus went into the wilderness "to be tempted" — to establish the principles of His ministry. After John was arrested, Jesus came to Galilee and began his ministry which lasted approximately 3 years.

With the stories of the flight to Egypt, baptism in the Jordan, and temptation in the wilderness, the gospel writers establish a theme which runs through much of their work: Jesus is the true Israel, repeating in His life the major events of Israel's history. What God had said in Israel He said again in Jesus Christ. He is the Word by which we know God.

Preaching the Kingdom

The theme of Jesus' message was "The time is fulfilled, and the kingdom of God is at hand; repent and believe in the Gospel" (Mark 1:15). He said it in many places and in a variety of ways. He constantly confronted people with the kingdom of God. Something new had come. There was Good News to be believed. God was here and He would rule. Return to Him!

People came to hear Jesus in large numbers because His news WAS good. He brought hope to people who were disillusioned with life. But Jesus had more to do than announce the possibility of new life. He had the task of creating a fellowship of people who would carry on the work of proclaiming the Good News. So He selected 12 men whom He trained and equipped for this mission. These disciples or learners accompanied Him for the remainder of His ministry and carried His message into the world after He died.

While they were being trained they not only heard Jesus speak but they saw Him demonstrate the fact that God was present and available to men. When some friends brought a paralyzed man to Jesus, he walked away with strong legs and a clear conscience because he was forgiven. That was good news to him!

Mark 2:1-12
Healing the Paralytic

When a woman of low reputation came to Him and knelt at His feet, she was accepted

Luke 7:36-50
Forgiving the Woman

by Him and went away at peace. Not only His disciples but Simon the Pharisee, in whose house He was dining, learned what forgiveness means.

When Jesus healed a man with dropsy on the Sabbath (there was a law against working on the Sabbath) the disciples learned that people are more important than traditions.

He taught always about the kingdom of God. His parables were stories showing what life is like when God is at the center of it as King. Sometimes He talked about the Kingdom directly. Sometimes He told stories which did not use the word but had a message about life

Luke 15:11-32
The Prodigal Son

with God. For example, He used the incident of a boy running away from home to show that we are like wayward children whose loving Father waits for us to return. Using an older brother theme in the same story He illustrated how sad it is when we jealously resent others who have benefited from God's grace.

Luke 18:10-14
The Pharisee and the
Tax Collector

In another story about two men who went to church, a "good" man with pride and a "bad" man with humility, He made it clear that the humble acceptance of mercy is the way for those who are in God's kingdom.

When He thought the disciples had caught a vision of what the Kingdom was about He tested them by asking: "Who do you say that I am?" Peter answered, "You are the Christ, the Son of the living God" (Matthew 16:13-20). Slowly the pieces of the puzzle were beginning to fit together. Yet it was not until after Christ's death and resurrection and the presence of His Spirit overtook them that His disciples felt confident to tell the world about Him.

All through His ministry Jesus continued to describe and illustrate what the new kind of life under God could be like. He wanted people to know that God is working to make what is broken whole; what is torn apart, at one; what is dead, alive. He gave people hope for the future by demonstrating that the future is in God's hands. He is in control. His kingdom is here and available to those who repent, that is, who are moved by grace to turn their lives around and see it.

Conflict

The Good News was not accepted by everyone. In the end we all rejected it. Jesus required sweeping changes. He insisted that priorities be shuffled. His kingdom of forgiving love had to come absolutely first, even before concern about food, clothing, or family (Matthew 6:25-33). He expected us to risk everything and live by trust in God rather than ourselves. He called us to adopt a discipline (discipleship) which would put life itself below God on the priority scale (Matthew 16:24-26). He said that life in the Kingdom is the only way to live, but it requires drastic changes in our reasons for living.

A man who talked like that was dangerous. He was a threat to every human way of life, to all man-made institutions and therefore to society as a whole. Those in authority in His day realized that Jesus threatened many time-hallowed traditions. They became increasingly frightened.

First they questioned His authority. "Now some of the scribes were sitting there questioning in their hearts, 'Why does this man speak thus? It is blasphemy! Who can forgive sins but God alone?' " (Mark 2:7). "And they said to Him, 'By what authority are You doing these things, or who gave You this authority to do them?' " (Mark 11:28)

They felt He kept the wrong kind of company. He must be a bad man. "The scribes of the Pharisees, when they saw that He was eating with sinners and tax collectors, said to His disciples, 'Why does He eat with tax collectors and sinners?'" (Mark 2:16)

They didn't like His interpretation of religious tradition. "And the Pharisees said to Him, 'Look, why are they [disciples] doing what is not lawful on the Sabbath?'" (Mark 2:24). "And the Pharisees and the scribes asked Him, 'Why do Your disciples not live according to the tradition of the elders?'" (Mark 7:5)

The hostility against Him continued to build. Various groups tried to trap Him into saying something which would destroy His reputation or lead to His arrest (Matthew 22:15 ff.). The people began to realize that His concept of a Kingdom was not the proud concept of dominion and prosperity they wanted, and they turned away from Him.

Jesus' Last Week

The conflict was bound to come to a head. There is every indication in the story that Jesus deliberately challenged every form of power in Jerusalem with His truth of equality and love. He forced the people to recognize the uncompromising demand of love—to accept His way or to kill Him and realize their shame.

Matthew 21:1-11
Palm Sunday

He entered the city of Jerusalem as a popular hero, with crowds cheering and waving branches, acclaiming Him as the Messiah king. When the leaders who knew He would not fulfill their hope of an earthly empire objected, He said, "I tell you, if these were silent the very stones would cry out."

He went to the temple and drove out the money changers and sacrifice sellers—on the Passover week when business reached its annual peak. He stood before the crowds in the temple and delivered a condemnation of the Pharisees—Israel's best people—so violent that He left them no shred of pride. When they came with questions to trap Him, He not only answered them but taunted them with their failure.

He disappointed the crowds who looked to Him as king. After the triumphal entry, they expected action. But He gathered no army; He gave no orders. He went back to friends in Bethany outside of Jerusalem every evening — and spoke of His burial to come. He did all of this during the preparation for Israel's feast of freedom, the Passover, when the longing for political freedom and the hatred of Rome reached fever pitch.

Mark 12:12-21
Passover Celebration

The disciples knew that the crisis was near. He sent two of them to prepare their Passover meal, which recalled the release of God's people from Egyptian bondage, in a large upper room in the city. Jesus and the Twelve sat down to eat the traditional meal together, even though Jesus was aware that one of them, named Judas, had betrayed Him to authorities. When Judas realized that Jesus knew what he was doing, he went out into the darkness.

"As they were eating, He took bread, and blessed, and broke it, and gave it to them, and said, 'Take; this is My body.' And He took a cup, and when He had given thanks He gave it to them, and they all drank of it. And He said to them, 'This is My blood of the covenant, which is poured out for many. Truly, I say to you, I shall not drink again of the fruit of the vine until that day when I drink it new in the kingdom of God.'" (Mark 14:22-25)

Jesus thus established the eating of a meal in and through which He gives Himself to people in order to renew the covenant which God has made with men. He took the ancient feast of deliverance and made it new in reference to Himself. He is now our celebration of freedom from bondage, a celebration Christians have observed for nearly 2,000 years.

When the meal was over and they had sung a hymn, Jesus and the disciples went out to the Mount of Olives, to a place called Gethsemane. Here Jesus spent much of the night struggling in prayer, "Father, all things are possible to Thee; remove this cup from Me; yet not what I will, but what Thou wilt." (Mark 14:36)

Mark 14:26-42
Gethsemane

Suddenly, Judas and the authorities and many others came. They led Jesus away. The disciples fled. Those who arrested Jesus took him first to the religious authorities, Annas and Caiaphas, for questioning. Because Palestine was under Roman rule, the religious authorities did not have the power to pass a death sentence. So Jesus was taken to Pilate, the Roman governor.

Matthew 27:11-27
Jesus Before Pilate

Pilate was as helpless as any before the challenge of Jesus. He found no fault, but his hatred and contempt for the Jews was so great that he could not speak peace. He taunted the mob, having Jesus whipped, and then calling Him their king. They cried out for Jesus' death and for the release of Barabbas, a rebel against Rome. So Pilate washed his hands of all responsibility and ordered the execution of Jesus. He was led out of the city to a place called Golgotha. There He was suspended on a post with His arms fastened to a crossbeam, along with two other prisoners. Crucifixion was the accepted method of execution at that time.

Luke 23:26-49
Jesus' Death

Luke 23:50-56
Burial

Jesus died that same day even though it was common for victims to endure the torture much longer. He was buried before sundown by some of His friends in a rockhewn tomb in a nearby garden. Since time was short, the task of preparing His body for burial was left unfinished. The women who assisted in

the burial planned to return after the Sabbath
to complete the task.

"And when the Sabbath was past, Mary
Magdalene, and Mary the mother of James,
and Salome, bought spices, so that they might
go and anoint Him. And very early on the
first day of the week they went to the tomb
when the sun had risen. And they were saying
to one another, 'Who will roll away the stone
for us from the door of the tomb?' And looking
up, they saw that the stone was rolled back;
for it was very large. And entering the tomb,
they saw a young man sitting on the right side,
dressed in a white robe; and they were amazed.
And he said to them, 'Do not be amazed; you
seek Jesus of Nazareth, who was crucified. He
has risen, He is not here; see the place where
they laid Him. But go, tell His disciples and
Peter that He is going before you to Galilee;
there you will see Him, as He told you.' And
they went out and fled from the tomb; for
trembling and astonishment had come upon
them; and they said nothing to any one, for
they were afraid." (Mark 16:1-8)

"Go into the World"

From one standpoint it appears Jesus was
nothing more than an unfortunate victim of
mob anger. But that is not the case. There was
a deliberateness about Jesus' actions that
indicates He did not blunder into His death but
went willingly. He had a mission. A man on
a mission has been sent by someone for
a reason. "For God so loved the world that He
gave His only Son, that whoever believes in
Him should not perish but have eternal life.
For God sent the Son into the world, not to
condemn the world, but that the world might
be saved through Him" (John 3:16, 17). God
was fulfilling his promise to Abraham that
through him and his descendants a great

blessing would come to the world. Jesus established a new covenant or testament with all who would trust in Him.

While most of the gospels end with various accounts of Jesus' appearing to His disciples, His story does not end here. It is difficult to reconstruct exactly what happened, but there is no doubt about the fact that His disciples underwent a great change in a very short time.

They were convinced Jesus was alive, and they had a directive from him: "Go therefore and make disciples of all nations, baptizing them in the name of the Father, and of the Son, and of the Holy Spirit, teaching them to observe all that I have commanded you; and lo, I am with you always, to the close of the age." (Matthew 28:19, 20)

On Pentecost, a Jewish festival which took place about 50 days after Jesus' death, His followers were together when they heard a sound like a mighty wind and they saw what appeared to be tongues of fire. Along with these symbols of the presence of God came a surge of power within them which moved them out into the streets to proclaim that "This Jesus whom you crucified, God has made Him both Lord and Christ" (Acts 2:36). The torch of this faith has been carried from nation to nation, from generation to generation. You are called to join the company of those who will not let it die.

THE CHRISTIAN CHURCH

The word church is used in a number of ways. It can refer to a building, a congregation, an organization, or to all believers in Christ. Here it means properly the whole movement known as Christianity, all those whom God has called as His agent of reconciliation on earth. It has its roots in the Old Testament people who were called by God to be a blessing to the world. The church is a new people under a New Covenant established by Christ. It has the same task of "going into the world," so that our God of grace might be known.

The fact that the church has survived and spread to nearly every nation is evidence of God's continuing activity in the world. Without God's power and initiative, the movement would have died or at least remained a religious sect within Judaism.

Challenges of the First Century

Many great barriers had to be overcome as Christianity spread from nation to nation, language to language, and culture to culture. Printing was unknown, the majority of people were uneducated, and most did not travel more than a few miles from their birthplace. From the very start there were problems. The handful of apostles and followers did not have a strategy for reaching the whole world. All they had was a tremendous experience and the conviction that it should be shared with others.

The *Acts of the Apostles* describes some of the difficulties they faced. As their number grew they had to develop a system for sharing responsibility (Acts 6). They faced harassment from the religious authorities. (Acts 4, 7, 9)

Two major questions of freedom had to be answered. The first was freedom from the ethnic limitations of the Jewish people. Through a vision given to Peter the church was led to include the Gentiles as equals. The second was freedom from the concept of Law (particularly the ritual laws of Judaism) as the way of salvation. Through Paul, apostle to the Gentiles, the church learned the power of grace above Law. But neither question has been forgotten, because racial conflict and the insistence on cultic ritual still plague many parts of the church.

The small minority of believers was often tempted to become discouraged and to revert to their old ways in the face of difficulties. But they were empowered by God Himself. "They were all filled with the Holy Spirit and spoke the word of God with boldness" (Acts 4:31b). Paul, the greatest missionary of the early church, said, "It was not I, but the grace of God which is with me." (Cf. 1 Corinthians 1−3)

When the church came into contact with the pagan world, questions arose concerning how to relate to unbelieving mates and neighbors. How free were Christians to live only by the law of love (1 Corinthians 7−8)? Abuses of the Lord's Supper were destroying the unity of the body of believers (1 Corinthians 11:20 ff.). The place of "speaking in tongues" had to be determined (1 Corinthians 14). Some were rejecting the very cornerstone of Christianity, the resurrection of the dead (1 Corinthians 15:12 ff.). False teachers soon arose who were leading the believers astray by saying the works of the Law took precedence over a faith relationship with Christ (see the Letter to the Galatians). Some lost confidence in the leadership and even suggested the apostle Paul was a fraud. 2 Corinthians 11:16 — 12:13 is Paul's defense of himself and an account of the hardships he suffered as a Christian. Finally, the New Testament records evidence of the persecution by the government. (1 Peter 4:12 ff.)

All of these problems and more faced the church before the end of the first century. It was not luck or brilliant maneuvers on the part of those common people which caused the church to spread. God was at work among them.

New Testament Writings

The New Testament was written out of necessity. As the original eye witnesses to Christ's life passed from the scene, it became necessary to record who Jesus is and how the church understands Him. The gospels of Matthew, Mark, Luke, and John recorded the events connected with Him and interpreted them in the Spirits' meaning. The Epistles, especially letters like the ones to the Romans, Ephesians, Colossians, and Hebrews, are statements of doctrine and ethics. These helped to preserve true teaching as divergent ideas and views arose. Some epistles, such as the Letters to the Corinthians, helped to establish and preserve practices consistent with the faith.

The writing of Scripture was one way God preserved the church and some degree of unity within it. Just as the giving of the Law served to keep the people of Israel in the Old Covenant, the New Testament writings helped to maintain people in the fellowship of Christ.

Later Challenges to the Church

The persecution of Christians in the Roman Empire reached its peak in the third and fourth centuries. However, by A. D. 325 Constantine declared Christianity legal. This must have looked like a real break for the church, but acceptance brought its own problems.

The Roman Empire declined as the power of the church

increased. The connection between the two grew as a result of the efforts of several rulers to strengthen the empire through an alliance with Christianity. Slowly the church adapted itself to the empire. What started out as an expression of the kingdom of God, detached from secular power, became part of a network of agencies of the world.

Vast political upheavals challenged the church. The Germanic tribes from the north invaded the empire, looking for land. They settled among the people but could not absorb the Roman civilization. The church remained intact and was accepted by the invading hordes. This further enhanced the political power and prestige of church leaders.

Eventually the bishop of Rome (pope) had powers similar to the emperor. By A. D. 800 Charlemagne was crowned by the pope and this alliance signaled the official beginning of the Holy Roman Empire. In theory the church and state were to cooperate as equals, but in fact the church often claimed to be superior.

The church now not only had unlimited power but it became involved in the feudal system and therefore owned much of the land, perhaps as much as one fourth of countries like Italy, France, Germany, and England. Church officials became feudal lords with power over the material as well as spiritual welfare of the people. Heavy taxes were collected by the church, making it extremely wealthy.

Early in the 7th century Mohammed began promoting his idea of one religion—a combination of pagan, Jewish, and Christian teachings. It spread rapidly, often by force, as his followers marched over Persia, Palestine, Syria, Asia Minor, North Africa, and Spain. Later the Turks became a similar threat to the church.

A cleavage between the Eastern Church and the Roman Catholic Church began in the 1st century. The contest of power was completed in A. D. 1054, when each church excommunicated the other.

From the very beginning the church was buffeted by external enemies and torn by internal conflict. It was divided by heresies, distracted by power and wealth, used for personal gain, attacked by enemies of all kinds and yet it endured! Its record is by no means clean. The Crusades, an attempt to recapture the Holy Land from the Turks, and the Inquisition, a program of wiping out heresy by exterminating those who disagreed, are two familiar and horrible blots on its history.

Yet God was able to work even during those "dark ages" to preserve the Scriptures, a people, and a heritage which made it possible for the church to continue. The church is holy only by the grace of God. Even when the church was at its worst, there were always those who were faithful to Christ and who exercised obedience at great cost. The true church (the people of God) was at times eclipsed by the political organization but it was there, wherever "two or three gathered together in His name."

Early Reformers

There had always been those who rejected the state-related, highly organized church but they were not strong enough to bring about any reform. In the 12th century the Waldenses, who declined wealth and went about preaching from the Bible, made some impact.

John Wyclif, who lived in England, was concerned about the ignorance and superstition of the people, so he translated the Bible into their language. His efforts were not appreciated. He died a peaceful death in 1384, but in 1428 his body was dug up and burned to show he had been considered a heretic.

In the next century a young man by the name of John Huss carried on Wyclif's ideas and denounced the wealth and corruption of the church. Though Huss was given a promise of safe conduct to appear at a council in 1414, when he arrived he was imprisoned and later burned at the stake.

Savonarola was an Italian critic of the church who was rewarded for his contribution by being tortured, hanged, and burned.

These are a few of the early reformers who lost their lives but laid wood on the pyre of the medieval church. Their followers were ready when the conditions were right and a man named Martin Luther struck the match of the 16th century reformation.

The Reformation

By the early 16th century, a number of social and political events had prepared the way for reformation of the church. Rising national consciousness helped political leaders to challenge the power of the pope. The threat of Turkish invasion in East Europe made peace in Western Europe mandatory. The Crusades had opened many minds to knowledge which questioned the dogmatic claims of the church, and trade with the East had greatly strengthened an independent middle class of people. The peasants heard of worlds beyond their villages and began to complain about feudal oppression. The need for change was widely felt and the invention of the printing press by Gutenberg in 1440 made possible the wide distribution of literature for the first time.

Luther was born November 10, 1483. His parents were peasants who taught him to work hard and be self-reliant. Martin's father wanted him to be an educated man, preferably a lawyer, so when he graduated from the University of Erfurt in 1505, he began the study of law. However, later that same year he entered an Augustinian monastery in an attempt to attain a holiness which would give him inner peace.

He had been reared in an atmosphere of fear and was taught that a totally religious life could guarantee him salvation. But his life as a monk did not bring the peace with God which he sought. Neither did his ordination into the priesthood. Even a pilgrimage to Rome (1510–1511) did not quiet his mind's conflict.

It was while he was a professor at the University of Wittenberg, lecturing on the Epistle to the Romans, that he recovered the Biblical concept of grace. He discovered that God was not determined to punish and destroy him but to offer life and hope in Christ. Through Him God had set things right and a person needed only to allow God to give him "life and salvation." Trusting God to do this is what the Bible means when it says, "For by grace you have been saved through faith; and this is not your own doing, it is the gift of God." (Ephesians 2:8)

Luther did not set out to change the church, but once he found the "Good News" he had to share it. On October 31, 1517, he nailed 95 theses or statements to the church door at Wittenberg and said he was willing to defend them in a debate. This date has come to mark the beginning of the Reformation.

Luther's theses challenged the power structures of the church by questioning its doctrine. But the political, social, and economic ferments were of such proportions that the Roman clergy were unable to remove his threat. In one sense, Luther stopped the revolution by providing a conservative leadership to the forces which were turning against the organized church.

He did not intend to found a new church—only to reform what was there. When this was obviously impossible, he accepted his excommunication by the pope and no longer looked to Rome for help. From Germany the reform movement soon spread to Switzerland, Scandinavia, England, and to a lesser degree to

France, Spain, and East Europe. John Calvin and Ulrich Zwingli were two important leaders in the 16th century.

For a number of reasons, the Reformation gave birth to many denominations. Differences in emphasis, interpretation, and practice arose with the new freedom of the age. Some groups came into being as a reaction to weaknesses in the existing church. John and Charles Wesley, for example, spoke against the cold formalism of the Anglican Church during the 18th century, and their protest resulted in the formation of the Methodist Church. Many of the other denominations have a similar history.

The church is today divided into several hundred denominations. The division has caused a great deal of bitterness and hate, yet even this variety has been useful in the economy of God. It has provided a way to meet the varied needs of people at different times. God has not been defeated by the foolishness of man. The church remains! People still gather around Christ as He reveals Himself in the Word and Sacraments. Men still seek to know and do His will. By His Spirit He continues to "call, gather, enlighten, and sanctify the whole Christian church on earth."

Lutherans in America

The Lutheran church came to America with the immigrants from Europe. Scattered and speaking different languages, the Lutherans really did not find each other until well into the 20th century. Some unification had taken place earlier within groups of the same national background, but it was not until 1960 that a merger took place which combined national heritages. This union of churches of Danish, Norwegian, and German background created The American Lutheran Church.

A series of mergers of synods, German and Swedish, which had been in this country for several centuries, culminated in the formation of the Lutheran Church in America in 1962.

The Lutheran Church—Missouri Synod, which was organized in 1846 by immigrants from Germany, became a body of over 2½ million members without benefit of mergers.

These three groups: The Lutheran Church in America (3 million), The Lutheran Church—Missouri Synod (2½ million), and The American Lutheran Church (2½ million) make up 95 percent of the Lutherans in this country. They cooperate in many kinds of work through an agency called the Lutheran Council in the United States of America.

"To This You Have Been Called"

The history of the church is a complex and in many ways dramatic story. The development of its doctrine and worship forms, its structure and organization, its contributions to the artistic and literary fields, its service to the sick, homeless, and hungry, and its efforts at education are some of the threads which must be woven together into the story of the church.

"The body of Christ" is one of the pictures which the New Testament gives us. Like Christ, the church is both human and divine. You can see its humanity, even from the outside. From within, it is possible to also see it as God's creation.

He invites all who will follow Christ to gather together around Him so that they can be sent into the world, equipped with the Spirit's gifts of "love, joy, peace, patience, kindness, goodness, faithfulness, gentleness, self-control." (Galatians 5:22)

You are called to be part of God's people.

BIBLIOGRAPHY

*Permission to quote from the works cited has been granted
by the following publishers*

American Bible Society. *Good News for Modern Man*. New York: American Bible Society, 1966.

Aulen, Gustaf. *The Faith of the Christian Church*. Philadelphia: Muhlenberg Press, 1948.

Bainton, Roland H. *Here I Stand*. Nashville: Abingdon Press, 1950.

Bainton, Roland H. (trans. and arranged by). *The Martin Luther Christmas Book*. Philadelphia: Muhlenberg Press, 1958.

Barclay, William. *The Making of the Bible*. Nashville: Abingdon Press, 1961.

Barclay, William. *The Mind of St. Paul*. New York: Harper & Brothers, Publishers, 1958.

Benet, Stephen Vincent. "Judgment" from *Ballads and Poems* in *Selected Works of Stephen Vincent Benet*. Copyright 1931 by Stephen Vincent Benet. Copyright 1959 by Rosemary Carr Benet. New York: Holt, Rinehart and Winston, Inc.

Bodensieck, J. *The Encyclopedia of the Lutheran Church* (N – Z). Minneapolis, Minn.: Augsburg Publishing House, 1965.

Bonhoeffer, Dietrich. *The Cost of Discipleship*. New York: The Macmillan Company, 1948.

Bonhoeffer, Dietrich. *Letters and Papers from Prison*. New York: The Macmillan Company, 1967 (revised).

Bonhoeffer, Dietrich. *Life Together*. New York: Harper & Brothers, Publishers, 1954.

Brandt, Leslie F. *Good Lord, Where Are You?* St. Louis: Concordia Publishing House, 1967.

Brokering, Herbert F., and Mark. *City and Country*. Philadelphia: Fortress Press, 1970.

Brokering, Herbert F. and Sister Noemi. *In Due Season*. Minneapolis, Minn.. Augsburg Publishing House, 1966.

Brokering, Herbert F. and Zimbolt, Joseph. *Lifetimes*. St. Louis: Concordia Publishing House, 1966.

Brokering, Herbert F. *Lord, Be With*. St. Louis: Concordia Publishing House, 1969.

Burtness, James H. *Whatever You Do*. Minneapolis, Minn.: Augsburg Publishing House, 1967.

Habel, Norman C. *For Mature Adults Only*. Philadelphia: Fortress Press, 1969.

Hordern, William E. *A Layman's Guide to Protestant Theology*. Revised ed. New York: The Macmillan Company, 1968.

Howard, Thomas. *Christ the Tiger*. New York: J. B. Lippincott Company, 1967.

Kallas, James. *A Layman's Introduction to Christian Thought*. Philadelphia: The Westminster Press, 1969.

Kantonen, T. A. *Life After Death*. Philadelphia: Muhlenberg Press, 1962.

Kennedy, Gerald H. *A Reader's Notebook*. New York: Harper & Brothers, 1953.

Khayyam, Omar. *Rubaiyat of Omar Khayyam,* trans. Edward Fitzgerald. New York: Random House, Inc., 1947.

Klos, Frank W. *Confirmation and First Communion:* A Study Book. Augsburg Publishing House, Board of Publication, LCA, Concordia Publishing House, 1968.

Lewis, C. S. *Christian Behavior.* New York: The Macmillan Company, 1945.

Lewis, C. S. *The Case for Christianity.* New York: The Macmillan Company, 1948.

Luther, Martin. *The Small Catechism.* Minneapolis, Minn.: Augsburg Publishing House; Philadelphia: Fortress Press, 1960.

• Marshall, Robert J. *The Mighty Acts of God.* Philadelphia: Lutheran Church Press, 1964.

Miller, Keith. *Habitation of Dragons.* Waco, Texas: Word Books, Publisher, 1970.

Paton, Alan. "Meditation for a Young Boy Confirmed" in *The Christian Century* (October 13, 1954). New York: Charles Scribners Sons.

Pierce, Edith Lovejoy. "Jesus Wrote With His Finger on the Ground," *The Christian Century* (July 16, 1958).

Plass, Ewald M. *What Luther Says,* Vols. I, II, III. St. Louis: Concordia Publishing House, 1959.

Quoist, Michael. *Prayers.* New York: Sheed & Ward, Inc., 1963.

The Report of the Joint Commission on the Theology and Practice of Confirmation. Minneapolis, Minn.: Augsburg Publishing House; St. Louis: Concordia Publishing House; Philadelphia: Board of Publication, Lutheran Church in America, 1970.

Rogness, Alvin. *Captured by Mystery.* Minneapolis, Minn.: Augsburg Publishing House, 1966.

Rogness, Alvin. *Forgiveness and Confession.* Minneapolis, Minn.: Augsburg Publishing House, 1970.

Schuller, David S. *Power Structures and the Church.* St. Louis: Concordia Publishing House, 1969.

Sherrill, Lewis Joseph, *Guilt and Redemption.* Richmond, Va.: John Knox Press, 1945.

Smart, James D. *The Rebirth of Ministry.* Philadelphia: The Westminster Press, 1960.

Smart, James D. *The Recovery of Humanity.* Philadelphia: The Westminster Press, 1953.

Streng, William D. *In Search of Ultimates.* Minneapolis, Minn.: Augsburg Publishing House, 1969.

Stringfellow, William. *A Private and Public Faith.* Grand Rapids, Mich.: William B. Eerdmans Publishing Company, 1962.

Theological Professors of The American Lutheran Church. *The Bible: Book of Faith.* Minneapolis, Minn.: Augsburg Publishing House, 1964.

Thielicke, Helmut. *Man in God's World.* New York: Harper & Row, Publishers, 1963.

Thielicker Helmut. *Our Heavenly Father.* New York: Harper & Brothers, Publishers, 1960.

Tournier, Paul. *A Place for You.* New York: Harper & Row, Publishers, 1968.

Tournier, Paul. *Guilt and Grace.* New York: Harper & Row, Publishers, 1958; English translation, 1962.

Vonnegut, Kurt Jr. *Cat's Cradle.* New York: Dell Publishing Company, 1963.

Webber, George W. *God's Colony in Man's World.* Nashville: Abingdon Press, 1960.

APPENDIX

This section contains worksheets and other items to be used in connection with the course. They will be used as directed by the leader of the class.

WHAT SHALL WE AIM FOR?

Below is a list of possible objectives for this course. Read over the list thoughtfully. Then check the *eight* statements you feel are the things you would most like to get out of this course.

By the time this course is finished, I would like to:

_____ A. Know the people in this class.

_____ B. Understand and be able to use more correctly some key words such as grace, sin, faith, salvation, Gospel, church, etc.

_____ C. Be able to study and interpret the Bible more readily.

_____ D. Have a better understanding of Biblical history.

_____ E. Know the distinct traditions and emphases of the Lutheran Church.

_____ F. Find significance in, and help for, daily life.

_____ G. Be able to put into words what I believe.

_____ H. Feel accepted by and involved in this congregation.

_____ I. Have a closer relationship with God in Christ.

_____ J. Understand myself better.

_____ K. Better understand the basic teachings of the Christian church.

_____ L. Be able to worship with more understanding and reverence.

_____ M. Make some new friends.

_____ N. Appreciate the Sacraments of Baptism and the Lord's Supper more fully.

_____ O. Be assured of eternal life.

_____ P. Be able to pray more confidently.

One evening several years ago I was taking a young friend out to dinner. He had just graduated from the university and was going off to enter the Christian ministry the next day. John was one of those fine, clean young men who somehow get through college without scar or blemish from the world. I found him hard to believe, but he was evidently sincere. We had eaten in a cafeteria and were talking about his future when a good-looking young woman sauntered up to our table in a pair of very short shorts, sandals, and one of those brief halter type tops. She was followed by a tiny daughter in a similar outfit. I recognized the woman as a member of the Sunday school class I taught. The class was rather large, and I had seen her only as a member of an audience. A few times I had spoken to her briefly before or after class, but I had definitely noticed her.

Somehow at the cafeteria, however, she looked very "un-Sunday schooly." I introduced her to my young friend as a fellow member of the same Sunday school class, and asked if she would like to join us. She did, and said at once, "There is something I've been wanting to talk to you about for months."

"What's that?"

"Paul, I think he was a sex deviate."

My young friend's eyes were protruding slightly in horror, and I sort of wished I had not asked.

"Paul who?" I asked, smiling weakly.

She laughed, "You know who I mean, Paul the Apostle."

So we began to talk about Paul's views concerning women and sex. After about 40 minutes it was apparent that Paul was not the problem she wanted to talk about, and I told her so.

Her whole attitude changed. She said almost wistfully, "I really believe you've found hope in your faith, and I would honestly like to make this beginning commitment of my life to Christ . . . but I can't do it."

"Why not?" I asked gently.

"Because I've got a personal problem that I can't seem to resolve." She was biting her lips and looking down at a paper napkin she had folded into a small bulky square.

"But that's why Christianity is called 'good news,'" I said, coming on strong. "We can't solve our own basic hang-ups and separations, and God is offering through the Holy Spirit to furnish us the motivating power to cope with the seemingly impossible situations in life. That's why I'm such a nut about Christianity. I can't promise to change anything. All I can do is to accept His love and grace."

"But," and she hesitated . . . "I don't feel acceptable until I whip this problem."

"Listen, Susan, the old song doesn't say, 'Just as I am when I whip my major problem.' It says, 'Just as I am without *one plea,'* one *problem,* one *guarantee."*

She looked at me with the strangest dawning look of hope. "Do you really believe that?" she said.

"I'd bet my life on it."

She looked down at her hands for several minutes. "All right," she said, almost as a challenge, "I'm committing adultery every Thursday night with a man who has a wife and several young children. And I *cannot* quit. Now can I come into your Christian family?"

I just looked at her. I certainly had not expected that. My first conditioned reaction as a Christian churchman would have been to think she is not ready for Christ, or to say something like, "Baby, don't you think you could at least cut down a little?"

Suddenly I realized how phony we Christians are. Of course we *would* expect her to quit committing adultery. We don't mean "just as I am without one plea." We actually mean, "Just as I am when I *promise* implicity to straighten up and quit my major sins." And this girl had nailed me with her honesty. She had heard the *real* intent of our church's congregational invitation and knew she did not have the strength to meet its requirements—to quit her "sinning." And yet it was her weakness which had brought her toward Christ in the first place.

I thought about Jesus and what He would have done. Then I looked up at her, "Of course, you can commit your life to Christ just as you are," I smiled. "He knows you want to quit seeing this man, and I don't know where else you can ever *hope* to find the security and strength to break up with him. So if you commit your life to Christ right now, then Thursday night, if you find you can't help meeting your friend, take Christ with you in your conscious mind through the whole evening. Ask Him to give you the desire and the strength to break off the relationship."

And she stepped across the stream and became a Christian.

Keith Miller, Habitation of Dragons, pp. 69—71

Letter to "you"—from a troubled teen-ager

Dear _____,

I'm not sure how you're going to take this letter, but I've been thinking about it a long time and am finally going to say it.

I'm having problems with the church—any church. That is, I no longer have any interest in church because I have such big questions about it—what's it for? What is it trying to do? I believe in God. I believe we need to teach right and wrong. But why have a church? It seems to demand a lot of money, time, and energy to keep it going—and what for? I'd certainly appreciate your thoughts on just what the church is and why we have it.

Sincerely,

WHAT IS THE CHURCH?

This worksheet is intended to help you think through your ideas on the nature and purpose of the church. Write the number which most nearly corresponds with your opinion regarding what the church actually is (column 1) and what it should be (column 2).

0 Totally disagree	3 Tend to agree
1 Disagree	4 Agree!
2 Tend to disagree	5 Totally agree!

The church   The church
    is   should be

_____   _____   Like a welfare agency — primarily concerned about the social problems of the community and world.

_____   _____   Like a visit to a counselor — to learn how to cope with life.

_____   _____   Like a social group — to develop fellowship.

_____   _____   Like a vacation — opportunity to get away and experience peace of mind.

_____   _____   Like a school — a place to learn important rules for living.

_____   _____   Like an airlines terminal — a place to get a ticket to eternity.

_____   _____   Like a court of law — a symbol of right and wrong to the community.

_____   _____   Like a (sales, company, staff) meeting — a time to hear from the Boss.

_____   _____   Like the Fourth of July — to remember and celebrate.

_____   _____   Like a broadcasting station — announcing good and bad news.

Indicate your reaction to the following statements by checking the appropriate blank (agree, unsure, disagree) before each statement.

Agree	Unsure	Disagree	
————	————	————	1. Man can talk with God.
————	————	————	2. Every page of the Bible is true.
————	————	————	3. God speaks to man apart from the Bible.
————	————	————	4. We can know the will of God through our interpretation of events.
————	————	————	5. God communicates through the Lord's Supper.
————	————	————	6. The Word of God could be made known without a Bible.

DISCUSSION STARTERS

1. Imagine this situation. There are 20 Christian churches in a small city and surrounding area. On a given Sunday all the pastors preach on precisely the same text from the Bible. What are the chances that every sermon will be identical? What are the chances that the sermons will be very different—and perhaps even contradictory? If the latter is true, where would the Word of God be preached and taught? At all churches? In some? How could you tell?

2. Someone has said, "Jesus loves me, this I know, for my mother told me so." What is your reaction? What does it say about the Word of God?

3. During the Napoleonic wars a group of soldiers went AWOL and hid out in a very secluded area, living off the land. They avoided contact with other persons for fear of detection, and so did not get news of the outside world. Consequently, they remained in hiding years after the war was over and peace was restored.

One day a messenger found them and announced, "The war is over. Peace is restored. The government has announced an amnesty, and you are free men!" He invited them to come out of hiding to enjoy the liberty which was theirs.

What should they do? What options do they have? What was required of them in order to enjoy the freedom they already had? What would keep them from claiming it? In what way does the messenger represent "the Word of God"?

SIX DESCRIPTIONS OF AN EVENT

The word was visible out there. The child, the scream, the looking,
the going part, the stopping. Some were going too fast to see everything.
But they saw and heard and imagined. All they knew was she was lost.
Her cheeks were red. They saw her fear.
And all she was saying was, "Mommie! Mommie! Mommie!"
Being lost is being hurt.
And all the mother needed was the cry. So familiar.
She heard and she came. She recognized the crying word.
Blinded by tears the girl knew the hug and the voice.
She was glad. Oh, was she glad.
The word is the way people care for each other.
If they will.

I direct my cries to the Lord.
Out of the ear-piercing sounds
and the ceaseless turmoil
of this concrete jungle
I speak God's name.
For my heart is deeply troubled and depressed,
and I feel weary and faint.

I am confused and lost.
I cannot find my way.
The nameless faces that flit by take no notice
of me.
No one knows my name,
And no one cares.

I turn to You, O God.
You have heard me before,
And You responded to my cries.
Perhaps even amidst the frustrating activity
and the crowded streets of the great city
You can hear the cries of a lonely child.

Excerpt from sermon

Yesterday, as I drove downtown in heavy traffic, I saw something which appalled me. Above the noise of the traffic I heard the piercing sounds of a child crying. Obviously she was lost, alone, afraid. People were passing by on all sides, but no one stopped to ask or be of comfort. It is indicative of the callous unconcern which people have for each other that they could coldly walk by a child in great need — too busy about their own affairs, too wrapped up in their own concerns to hear the cries of a lost child.

Newspaper report — simple narrative

A small flurry of excitement occurred this morning at the corner of Cedar and First Street when 5-year-old Cindy Martin let out a scream that scared passersby for a moment. It seems that Cindy momentarily lost track of her mother at about the time an ambulance went screeching past. This proved to be too much for little Cindy, and she let out a piercing scream which caused those around to wonder who had been hurt. The crisis passed. Mother was reunited with Cindy and all is well.

Letter from child's mother to her parents

Dear Folks,

Yesterday was a traumatic day. I took Cindy downtown shopping with me. As I was busy talking to a clerk, I became suddenly aware that Cindy wasn't around. Just as I was beginning to look for her, I heard the sound of an ambulance siren. You can imagine that my heart sank and I began to panic. I was sure that she had been hit by a car. As I rushed out of the store, all I could see was a crowd of people and I could hear Cindy screaming.

You can imagine my relief when I discovered that she had become lost, and her screams were because she was afraid, not because she was hurt.

It made me thankful to God to have her alive and well. It also shocked me into keeping better watch over her when we go shopping.

Descriptive

A small girl is standing on a sidewalk near a busy street. People are standing around her or are walking by. She is wearing a light colored knit dress. She has blond hair fixed in a pony tail. She has her hands over her ears and has her mouth open wide. The pavement on which she is standing is cracked and seems to have been recently repaired.

WRITING THE

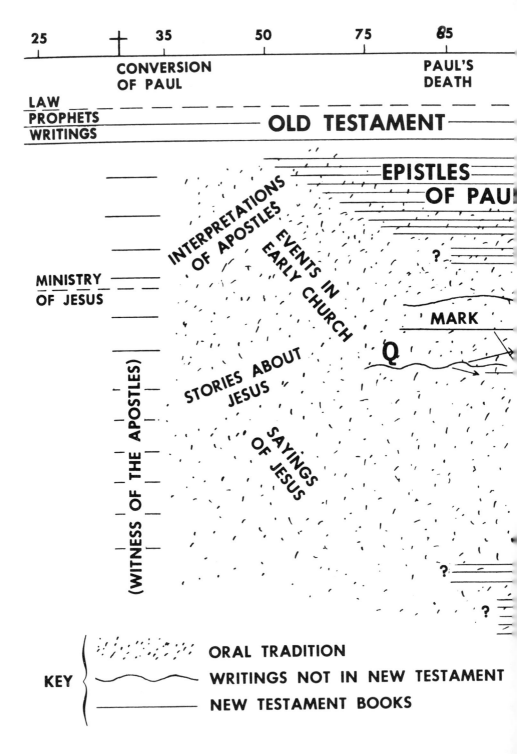

| 25 | | 35 | | 50 | | 75 | | 85 |

CONVERSION
OF PAUL

PAUL'S
DEATH

LAW
PROPHETS
WRITINGS

OLD TESTAMENT

EPISTLES
OF PAUL

INTERPRETATIONS
OF APOSTLES

EVENTS IN
EARLY CHURCH

MINISTRY
OF JESUS

?

MARK

Q

STORIES ABOUT
JESUS

SAYINGS
OF JESUS

(WITNESS OF THE APOSTLES)

?

?

KEY

ORAL TRADITION

WRITINGS NOT IN NEW TESTAMENT

NEW TESTAMENT BOOKS

NEW TESTAMENT

100	125	150

ASTORAL EPISTLES

Other Gospels

JKE — ACTS
MATTHEW

Didache

OHN

Shepherd of Hermas

1 Clement

Barnabas

NERAL
EPISTLES

Revelation of Peter

REVELATION OF JOHN

YOU — DEATH — HOPE

1. When you were a child, how was death talked about in your family?
   ____ a. Openly.
   ____ b. With some sense of discomfort.
   ____ c. Only when necessary and then with an attempt to exclude the children.
   ____ d. As though it were a taboo subject.
   ____ e. Never recall any discussion.

2. How often do you think about your own death?
   ____ a. Very frequently.
   ____ b. Frequently.
   ____ c. Occasionally.
   ____ d. Rarely (no more than once a year).
   ____ e. Very rarely or never.

3. What aspect of your own death is the most distasteful to you? Rate the three most significant to you.
   ____ a. I could no longer have any experiences.
   ____ b. I am afraid of what might happen to my body after death.
   ____ c. I am uncertain as to what might happen to me if there is a life after death.
   ____ d. I could no longer provide for my dependents.
   ____ e. It would cause grief to my relatives and friends.
   ____ f. All my plans and projects would come to an end.
   ____ g. The process of dying might be painful.
   ____ h. Other (specify): _____

4. Has there been a time in your life when you wanted to die?
   ____ a. Yes, mainly because of great physical pain.
   ____ b. Yes, mainly because of great emotional upset.
   ____ c. Yes, mainly to escape an intolerable social or interpersonal situation.
   ____ d. Yes, mainly because of great embarrassment.
   ____ e. Yes, for a reason other than the above.
   ____ f. No.

5. If your physician knew that you had a terminal disease and a limited time to live, would you want him to tell you?
   ____ a. Yes.
   ____ b. No.
   ____ c. It would depend on the circumstances.

6. What kind of funeral would you prefer?
   ____ a. Burial.
   ____ b. Cremation.
   ____ c. Donation to medical school or science.
   ____ d. Whatever my survivors want.
   ____ e. None.

7. To what extent do you believe in a life after death?
    ____ a. Strongly believe in it.
    ____ b. Tend to believe in it.
    ____ c. Uncertain.
    ____ d. Tend to doubt it.
    ____ e. Convinced that it does not exist.

8. Regardless of your belief about life after death, what is your wish about it?
    ____ a. I strongly wish there were a life after death.
    ____ b. I am indifferent as to whether there is a life after death.
    ____ c. I definitely prefer that there not be a life after death.

9. What do you feel about life after death and a glorious end to the world?
    ____ a. It was easier to believe in it in Biblical days than now.
    ____ b. It is easier to believe now than in Biblical days.
    ____ c. It's about the same now as in Biblical days.

10. Regarding my situation after death —
    ____ a. I am somewhat fearful about it.
    ____ b. I wonder about it sometimes.
    ____ c. I rarely if ever think about it.
    ____ d. I am very confident and cheerful about it.
    ____ e. I am sometimes fearful and sometimes cheerful.

11. How do you expect to die?

12. Describe your funeral.